THE TRIUMPH OF SATAN

THE TRIUMPH OF
satan

Harry E. Wedeck

THE CITADEL PRESS
SECAUCUS, NEW JERSEY

First paperbound printing, 1974
Copyright © 1970 by Harry E. Wedeck
Published by Citadel Press
A division of Lyle Stuart, Inc.
20 Enterprise Ave., Secaucus, N.J. 07094
In Canada: George J. McLeod Limited
73 Bathurst St., Toronto 2B, Ontario
Manufactured in the United States of America
ISBN 0-8065-0422-6

⚜ contents ⚜

⚔ pREfACE ⚔

THIS BOOK tells the story, sometimes grim and awesome, occasionally lighter in vein and even whimsical, of Satan and his activities and impact on human beings. His influence ranges from the time that he lost his celestial status and began, in his humiliation and resentment, to retaliate on man, down to the rich and fertile field of operations in which he is now exulting.

Satan has been continuously a dominant figure, penetrating into public and domestic life, into political alignments, into the chaste customs and meditations of saintly women and holy anchorites, into the minds of the devout and righteous. He has promoted lascivious and unprincipled lusts and desires. He has maneuvered and cajoled, tricked and seduced by his snares and his protean capacities. All folklore, every legend is stamped with his sinister personality. He has entwined himself into conversation and ordinary speech, into dramatic situations, into opera and diabolic melodies, into pictorial and sculptural representations, into chronicles and memoirs of all sorts.

So notable a character merits emphatic recognition as a forceful agent in the human scene. This survey proposes to give the Archfiend a due measure of such recognition.

H. E. W.

1

SATAN'S NAMES, HIS REALITY,
HIS CHARACTER

THE DEVIL is always with us—a pervasive, sinister, haunting figure. He appears in the earliest sagas and folklore of every nation, from Egypt to Babylonia, from the Nordic regions to the remote islands of the Pacific. He generates evil. He is evil incarnate. As the supreme Devil who has created turmoil and havoc throughout the ages of living man, he may well be proud of his status. For he stands as the adversary of God and of man. Yet there are times in the historical cycle when Satan seems to have shown glimpses of humanity. He may well do so at will, for he has ambivalent traits. He can assume a seductive tone. Or he startles with his menacing shape. He can inspire terror. He can cajole and intrigue. He can be man or beast. Again, he turns into some nameless, amorphous creature issuing from his bestial haunts. Hence, by virtue of this capacity for change, he has been called the Infernal Proteus. That was the age-old legend that followed the Satanic theme: his dramatic power to appear in an unexpected form. In Shakespeare's *Hamlet,* for example, a devil is regarded as capable of changing instantly into any desired shape:

> The spirit that I have seen may be a devil; and the devil hath power t'assume a pleasing shape.

In remote centuries the God Jehovah was one of many deities who were worshiped by the peoples of the Near East. Marduk and Cybele and the ancient Assyro-Babylonian deities were so dominant in the Mesopotamian regions that they usurped and absorbed the rites and ceremonies and liturgies of contending deities. Even the Semitic people who became the Israelites turned willing ears to the seductive glorification of these divinities and their obscene cults. But in time Jehovah came to assume ultimate superiority as the one God of the Jews.

At some later, indeterminate time, the concept of God assumed wholly and exclusively virtuous and beneficent features. God was wholly good, and all his acts were equally directed toward the welfare of man. All nonvirtuous attributes were discarded. And the malefic characteristics that remained were assigned to another form, an independent Satanic symbol. This Satanic form became the enemy of the benevolent God and likewise of God's creation, mankind.

In the early years of their history, the Israelites sacrificed a goat to Azazel, the demon of the desert. The term Azazel stems from *aziz*, strength, and *El*, God: hence, *the strength of God*. This Azazel, as we find him in Biblical literature, lost his character as the strong God and was no longer beneficent. He was a concept of evil, a Satanic symbol. In this evil aspect, as the repository of human transgressions, he appears in *Leviticus* 6:21–22:

> And Aaron shall lay both his hands upon the head of the live goat, and confess over him all the iniquities of the children of

Israel, and all their sins, putting upon them the head of the goat, and shall send him away by the hand of a fit man into the wilderness:
And the goat shall bear upon him all their iniquities unto a land not inhabited; and he shall let go the goat in the wilderness.

Retaining this goat-image, the medieval mind conceived Satan as a goat, horned and hoofed. He appears thus in the strange rite of the Sabbat—a mysterious, compulsive figure.

Satan's names are multiple, largely descriptive and condemnatory, but not exclusively so. And each designation points to some particular characteristic of the Fiend—his personal ways, his lineage, his intentions, his activities among men.

The term *Devil* stems, through the Latin *diabolus,* from the Greek διάβολος. The Greek word itself originally meant a slanderer, as Aristotle, for instance, uses the expression. In the Septuagint and the Greek Testament, it is equivalent to the Hebrew Satan, the adversary *par excellence.*

Biblical synonyms for Satan include Apollyon, Abaddon, Beelzebub, Belial. Apollyon denotes the *destroyer,* as the term appears in *Revelation* 9:11:

And they had a king over them, which is the angel of the bottomless pit, whose name in the Hebrew tongue is Abaddon, but in the Greek tongue hath his name Apollyon.

In the same context Abaddon means *destruction.* Beelzebub signifies *lord of flies,* to whom a temple was dedicated by the Canaanites. Belial means *without a master.* As Asmodeus, again, Satan is a *creature of judgment.* As Behemoth, he is the *Beast,* and the *Beast* was anciently the crocodile but in some contexts the hippopotamus. Diabolus itself is taken to mean *two morsels,* for he "kills the body and the soul." As the Demon, Satan is *cunning with blood.* As

Mephistopheles, "wandering in darkness," as John Trithemius, the medieval demonographer described him, he is the arch adversary in the Faust legend. According to one Greek etymology, Mephistopheles is "he who does not love light." Dante gives him sovereignty, calling him Emperor of the Doleful Kingdom. He is the Prince of Darkness and he is the Prince of this world. In the folklore of many peoples, this Evil Spirit assumes an animal form, and Satan becomes incarnate, particularly in the serpent, the goat, the cat, and the wolf.

The term *Devil* or the *Devil,* it should be noted, is a synonym for Satan. In the plural, the expression *devils* generally refers to the diabolic ministrants. In apocalyptic literature, in the *Testaments of the Twelve Patriarchs,* Satan has still more appellations: Belial, Sammael, Mastema, Azazel. Among the nations of the Near East and the Orient, the nomenclature of the Spirit of Evil varies but remains identical in its essential connotation. In Russian he becomes Tchort. The Persians know him as Dev. To Islam he is Iblis. Like the Biblical Satan, Iblis too was expelled from high heaven. In Syria they call him Béherit. The Arabs refer to him as Al Shaitan. In ancient Egypt he was the evil Set, who destroyed his brother Osiris. To the Japanese he was O Yama. The Koran calls him Satan. In the Zoroastrian religion of ancient Persia, the Evil Spirit was Angra Mainya. Again, in the cult of Mithra the Sun God, the supreme Evil Spirit, who was akin to Satan in his intent and his operations, had under his control a host of obscene demons who were sent forth to try to frustrate Mithra's creation of all beneficent beings upon the earth.

In the epic of the heroic Gilgamesh, king of Uruk in Mesopotamia, Destiny, in its grim and disastrous aspect, is called Namtar. Namtar is virtually the Satanic essence. He is conceived as a demon dwelling in the Nether World. He is the harbinger of pestilence and disease. In India he becomes Mrtya and, later on, Mara. He is the spirit of Death. With sublime arrogance he attempted to undermine the holy Buddha. In Brahmanism, Hiranyaksha is the demon who threatens to destroy the entire universe. The ancient Greeks, in their multiform mythology, represented Evil as Typhon, god of death and darkness. An angelic figure initially, and subsequently condemned by the Ultimate Power, Satan is regarded in mimetic attitude, imitating the Divinity, like an ape. In the medieval devotional manual entitled *The Ancren Riwle,* in fact—The Rule of Anchoresses—the Fiend is designated as the Old Ape.

In the New Testament the name Satan appears thirty-four times, while the expression Devil occurs thirty-six times. In the New Testament also, Satan is termed the dragon. Cyprian, the Bishop of Africa, so called him, in addition to the theologically condemnatory appellations of the ancient serpent, the enemy, the god of this world. The city of Pergamum is called in *Apocalypse* 2:13 the Throne of Satan, on account of its numerous idolatrous shrines.

In *Ephesians* 2:2, Satan is descriptively "The Prince of the Air." As the Prince of the Air, he is associated with light: hence, as Isaiah calls him, he is Lucifer, the Lightbearer.

But not so with Satan's minions, as *Ephesians* 6:12 depicts them:

> For we wrestle not against flesh
> and blood, but against
> principalities, against powers, against
> the rulers of the darkness
> of this world, against spiritual
> wickedness in high places.

It is not surprising, of course, to find the Satanic image recurrent in Biblical contexts. For Satan is the primal and everlasting enemy of the Sacred Books.

Satan first appears as an individualized personality, the enemy of man and the accuser before God, in *Zechariah* 3:ɪ–2. Satan, sitting in judgment, is the accuser of the high priest Joshua. He tries to disqualify Joshua for his high priestly duties and obstructs his entrance into the holy of holies on the day of the New Year:

And he shewed me Joshua the high priest standing before the angel of the Lord, and Satan standing at his right hand to resist him.

And the Lord said unto Satan, The Lord rebuke thee, O Satan; even the Lord that hath chosen Jerusalem rebuke thee; is not this a brand plucked out of the fire?

The last Biblical passage in which Satan appears is 1 *Chronicles* 21:1. Satan here plays the part of God. God sends a pestilence against Israel, and this pestilence is the work of the Evil One:

And Satan stood up against Israel, and provoked David to number Israel.

In the introductory chapters of *Job*, too, in 1:6–12, Satan, appearing before the Lord, is permitted to tempt Job:

Now there was a day when the sons of God came to present themselves before the Lord, and Satan came also among them.

And the Lord said unto Satan, whence comest thou? Then Satan answered the Lord and said, From going to and fro in the earth, and from walking up and down in it.

And the Lord said unto Satan, Hast thou considered my servant Job, that there is none like him in the earth, a perfect and an upright man, one that feareth God, and escheweth evil?

Then Satan answered the Lord, and said, Doth Job fear God for nought?

Hast not thou made an hedge about him, and about his house, and about all that he hath on every side? thou hast blessed the work of his hands, and his substance is increased in the land.

But put forth thine hand now, and touch all that he hath and he will curse thee to thy face.

And the Lord said unto Satan, Behold, all that he hath is in thy power; only upon himself put not forth thine hand. So Satan went forth from the presence of the Lord.

In *Revelation* 12:3–12, there is another account of Satan as the dragon, cast out of heaven:

And there appeared another wonder in heaven; and behold a great red dragon, having seven heads and ten horns, and seven crowns upon his heads.

And his tail drew the third part of the stars of heaven, and did cast them to the earth: and the dragon stood before the woman which was ready to be delivered, for to devour her child as soon as it was born.

And she brought forth a man child, who was to rule all nations with a rod of iron: and her child was caught up unto God, and to his throne.

And the woman fled into the wilderness where she hath a place prepared of God, that they should feed her there a thousand two hundred and threescore days.

And there was war in heaven: Michael and his angels fought against the dragon: and the dragon fought and his angels,

And prevailed not; neither was their place found any more in heaven.

And the great dragon was cast out, that old serpent, called the Devil, and Satan, which deceiveth the whole world: he was cast out into the earth, and his angels were cast out with him.

And I heard a loud voice saying in heaven, Now is come salvation, and strength, and the kingdom of our God, and the power of his Christ: for the accuser of our brethren is cast down, which accused them before our God day and night.

And they overcame him by the blood of the Lamb, and by the word of their testimony; and they loved not their lives unto the death.

Therefore rejoice, ye heavens, and ye that dwell in them.

Woe to the inhabiters of the earth and of the sea! for the devil
is come down unto you, having great wrath, because he knoweth
that he hath but a short time.

Whatever his local or ethnic name, the Satanic spirit does
not change its spots. Among Tibetans the demon is known
as Kha's Groma. The Tibetans even have a Devil's Altar, an
indication of his status. Gypsies call God devel, probably from
the Sanskrit term *deva,* the shining one.

In Japan there is a demon of lightning and a demon of
thunder.

The Musée Guimet in Paris has a collection of figures,
objects, and manuscripts relating to primitive religious cults
and practices. Here may be found many items associated
with the Satanic concept of pervasive, universal Evil. But
France is sometimes indulgent, and sees the Fiend in an in-
viting light. In Gascony, for instance, the Devil is revered
as a patron, and is known as Seigneur Voland.

As a patron, the Devil can be serviceable to man, provided
he is approached properly. In Madagascar, for example, the
Spirit of Evil is Nyang. He is all-powerful, and it is in-
cumbent to invoke his favor, as the following supplication
implies:

> O Nyang, bad and strong spirit,
> let not the thunder roar over
> our heads!
>
> Tell the sea to keep within
> its bounds!
>
> Spare, O Nyang, the ripening fruit
> and dry not up the blossoming rice!

In his climactic eminence, the Devil has his assistants, his
administrators, dispersed in strategic positions to implement
his injunctions. Occasionally, in legend and chronicle, a

sense of ridicule, of clownish belittlement, is attached to this Satanic corps of Foreign Service. The intention is evidently to bring Satan down to an earthly level, to poke fun at him and his creatures, and so to tear away the awesome aura that normally surrounds his manifestations. In the *Inferno,* for instance, Dante gives the attendant devils the fantastic character of imps performing in some theatrical pantomime. And equally grotesque are the humorous names he assigns to them: Ciriatto and Dragnignazzo, Farfarello, Rubicante, Scarmiglione, Grafficane, Alcobrina, Barbariccia, Alichino. Demoniac beings can never preserve their dignity under such names. A similar situation occurs in other areas. In England Satan is called, with a touch of scornful contempt, Gooseberry, or The Old Gentleman. More vulgarly, which means more boldly, he becomes Old Harry, Old Scratch, Old Horny, or Old Nick. In French he is the Sly One, Le Malin, but in Spanish a little dignity is added to Don Martin.

Through the centuries the Church Fathers, professional theologians, and exegetes who commented on Biblical texts all devoted time and effort to ponder over the conception of Satan's essential nature. He became the subject of passionate discussion and exposition. Many issues were raised and challenged. What was the primary reason for his fall? What was the immediate cause of his expulsion? Did he, as some speculators suggested, attempt to equate himself with the Creator of all things, the ultimate Being, the *mobile immobile*—he who creates but is not created himself? Did he go further, questioning the primacy of the Divinity? Why his persistent resentments against both God and man? Who were his satellites? What was their nature? What were their functions?

These and similar inquiries were for a long time confined to subjective considerations. They were more or less in the nature of academic themes. Satan, it was asserted, had no objective external reality or existence at any period. He was merely a concept, an idea, like the philosophical ideas expounded by Plato.

It is remarkable to observe how abundant and varied is the testimony on the Satanic topic, on the pervasive fact of evil. Evidence appears in the most anciently recorded religious doctrines of Egypt and Syria, of Hellenic paganism, of Roman polytheism, on through evolving Christianity and its exponents, down into the Middle Ages. Satan, in his ominous manifestations, was a dynamic figure, but still not palpable, still a concept. The Apostolic Fathers, Papias and Justin Martyr, Tatian and Athenagoras, considered him as the principal enemy of Christianity, against whom there must be constant, watchful resistance. He is the Evil One, the Black One. He is the Active One. And he combines in himself every pernicious element conceivable that tends to bring havoc on mankind.

The dominant personality of Augustine wrestles with him, and crushes him with his sheer sublime faith. Jerome confronted him, and many a Church Father made him the subject of preaching and writing, of polemics and exposés. The roster of such militant churchmen is long and distinguished, and eminent among them stand Ambrose and Anselm, Gregory and Cyprian, Clement and Origen. And yet the prideful nature of the arch enemy remained resilient, almost indurated, unassailable in many respects. The controversies and disputations to which he gave rise were strictly theological, confined to a comparatively small circle—churchmen, cultured men who interested themselves in theological and metaphysical problems as an intellectual activity. But they dealt in thought, in notions, not in pragmatic realities. Hence Satan was still at large, growing slowly into more than a notion, yet not circumscribed by defined terms, by delimitations.

And even as a concept, Satan provoked conflicting views

and opinions on his nature. Tertullian, the Church Father who flourished in the second century, says of him that he was born the wisest of all the angels before becoming the Devil. In the same vein *Ezekiel* (28:5) declares that Satan was originally created good and became evil by his own will:

Thou wast perfect in thy ways from the day that thou wast created, till iniquity was found in thee.

Lactantius, a fourth-century Christian writer on theological and polemical subjects, propounds another theory. God, he postulates, created a spirit like himself, compact of his own divine attributes. Then God created another being in whom the divine virtue was lacking. This being, jealous of his elder brother, was at first a beneficent spirit, but his jealousy drove him into wickedness.

The hieratic cult of the Phrygian Cybele, the Mighty Mother of the Gods, and the cults associated with Astarte and Demeter, with Isis and Osiris and a host of lesser or more obscure deities, were spiritual, religious phenomena. So the cult of the diabolic power, in its pervasive manifestation, had its exultant votaries. The Satanic dedication, in its conceptual form, was timeless, coeval with man.

Through the ages, in the second millennium B.C. and no less during the Dark Ages of the first five or six centuries of this era, Satanism was an influential, pervasive cult. This cult involved thaumaturgic performances, necromantic rites, blasphemous liturgies. It was a cult dedicated to the infernal powers and to their efficacy in triumphant evil. And even when Christianity, evolving in the early centuries, became established and codified in its theological canons, Satanism continued its stubborn opposition. It was not vanquished. It went underground, surviving in obscure forms in the hinterlands, in distant and isolated rural areas, among men and women who transmitted the traditional secrets of antique beliefs, and in the very essence of folklore, the oral, unwritten, but persistent records of man's views and speculations and interpretations of the universe.

Even during the fifteenth, sixteenth, and seventeenth centuries, when the enlightened Renaissance spread from Italy to France, to Britain and Spain, and to the Scandinavian and Slavic countries, man could not thrust or eject the Archfiend from his consciousness. He was entwined in men's meditations, in their commercial and urban affairs, in their domestic and social life, in their national awareness. Satan, in fact, was so dominant, so ubiquitous in his impacts on peasant and duke, on burgher and monk, that Church and State made strenuous efforts to outlaw him by thunderous punitive ordinances, to disband his devotees, to stamp out his sinister and disastrous seductions.

But even if Satan proved to be and actually were a phantasmal myth, an imaginative projection of the human mind, a hypothetical embodiment of rooted belief, he has imposed himself from the beginning of time to the present day with such insistence, so formidably and so tyrannically, that man no longer is really concerned about his actuality. By thinking so, man has given him actuality, material form. The Fiend's physical existence is no longer relevant. For Satan has achieved his task through his unsubstantial negativeness. He has willed himself to be among men and to induce a profound faith in his corporeal being, in the effectiveness of his infernal connivances, his cosmic scene of operations, his dark demotic theater of war.

To people at large, to the ordinary unnamed member of society, to folk living on a plane lower than the philosophers, to the unlettered and frequently quite lettered masses, to those removed from the major centers of culture and spiritual atmospheres, Satan is real. He has continuously possessed that very palpable reality. And even the speculative and philosophical spirit has at times been chary of definitively repudiating and denying his existence. Satan on occasion may become invisible, but he is always immanent, unceasingly permeating the entire universe. Salvian, a Christian writer of the fifth century, asserts with categorical conviction: *Ubique daemon*—Satan is everywhere. In the third century Diogenes Laertius, author of a compendium of Greek philosophy, points out that Heraclitus, a pre-Socratic philosopher, declared: "Every region on earth is filled with spirits and demons." Steeped in the Faustian atmosphere, Goethe, in confirmation of Satan's actuality, syllogizes:

> Ich kann mich nicht bereden passen,
> Macht mir den Teufel nur nicht klein:
> Ein Karl, den alle Menschen hassen,
> Der muss was sein!

> I cannot be convinced
> about underestimating the
> Devil.

> A creature that all men hate
> Must have some existence.

Thus, with mankind's assurances, Satan marches forward, increasing in stature, extending his impacts. In his machinations, in his probing investigations over the earth and under the waters, among men and beasts and strange amorphous elementals, he finds his satisfying fulfillment. All wealth, both hidden in inaccessible secrecy as well as known treasure, can be manipulated by him for his own ends. He can devastate cities in an instant. He can ruin nations with his will. He can create such universal chaos that entire populations are wiped out by war and plague and famine, by flood or earthquake. He is known to be the author of such cataclysms. Yet he remains largely invulnerable, triumphant in his schemes, perpetually contriving new agonies and fresh torment for mankind. The long, tortuous, and dire record of human history is manifest testimony to his share in man's blind plight.

Yet, strangely enough, in some instances his satellites have not always been malefic in their operations. They were essentially of service, for example, to King Solomon. Solomon was reputed to have dominion over the demons. His magic traveling carpet and his knowledge of the language of animals were the result of his demoniac mastery. These spirits, the legends ran throughout every land of the Orient, built his temple without tools, overnight. They taught him occult lore. From them he learned the arts of divination. Seated on his carpet, attended by Satanic creatures, he swept through the universe, master of the cosmos. All that he acquired, the totality of his knowledge, was imprinted later in his mystic manuals, his portentous grimoires, guides to the Occult World.

There is no end to Satan's occupations. He is the master architect, and his achievements include towers and castles and churches, but his forte seems to be the construction of bridges. Many bridges in European countries are traditionally linked with him, and are known as The Devil's Bridge. Coves of quaint formation, sheer precipices, hills and streams in sparsely populated areas are attributed to his handiwork and are associated, for identification, with his name.

Not only can the Evil One perform superhuman tasks, but he is capable of conquering nature itself. On the testimony of Tertullian, Satan could even carry water in a sieve.

Night is his climate. Then he is at his most effective pitch. Primarily he is a nocturnal being, and the dark of the night is most propitious for his enterprises. For at cockcrow, when the rooster, traditionally inimical to demoniac creatures, utters his shrill call to dawn, Satan vanishes, abortive and ineffectual. Light is, in all the ancient cults, the context for what is beneficent, while darkness invites whatever is evil.

In the "Hymn at Cockcrow," a poem by the Christian Latin poet Prudentius (348–c. 405 A.D.), the cock is the Christian symbol representing Christ.

This sums up the general view of this cosmic figure who bestrides mankind, who exists not only as a concept, a thought, an intellectualized image, but on a very earthly level, occupying space, possessed of autonomous decisions, girt, by the very nature of his being, for unending warfare. For Satan's fall was not his final catastrophe. His downfall from the supernal heights did not crush or even frustrate his designs, his contrived intentions. He was merely entering on a new phase, a fresh stage in his evolutionary progress.

Isaiah had already noted Satan's fall as a kind of interlude. For Satan, as the prophet saw, would not accept defeat. He was resolved to regain his heavenly seat:

> How art thou fallen from heaven,
> O Lucifer, son of the morning! . . .
> For thou hast said in thine heart,
> "I will exalt my throne
> above the stars of God!
> I will sit also upon
> the mount of the congregation . . .
> I will ascend above the heights
> of the clouds: I will be like the most High."
> Yet thou shalt be brought down to hell.

That is Isaiah's final thunderous prediction. When he addresses Satan as Lucifer, he recalls the primal angelic figure, Lucifer, the Lightbearer, the Biblical Promethean benefactor of mankind turned enemy.

In a sense, man is Satan's prisoner. And Satan is perpetually watchful to assault human defects when they are at a low ebb, incapable of resistance. For Satan, in his presumptuous arrogance, in his blazing rancor, claims all mankind as his domain. He claims the entire creation, in fact, as his own operation. The poet Prudentius describes this purpose of Satan in his *Hamartigenia*. Here he relates the conflict between Christians and demons, the unseen powers under Satan's rule. In a dream state, a certain Perpetua has a violent bout with the Devil. Christians, asserts Prudentius, are wrong to think that the struggle is with flesh and blood and palpitating veins and foul bile. No, we are at war day and night with the Spirits of Darkness, who rule the moist air that is dense with slow-moving clouds.

Yet, for all Satan's vast presumption, there appears an odd, almost domestic, note in his activities. For he has a mate, a female counterpart of evil. In *Paradise Lost,* Milton presents Satan with a daughter-wife. When the Evil One commits incest with her, their issue is Death. Dennis Wheatley, a British novelist who has written prolifically on occult themes, has published a novel entitled *To the Devil—a Daughter.*

The imaginative concept of Satan as a *persona* has, in the course of the centuries, undergone a variety of changes. Milton presents an awe-inspiring figure in *Paradise Lost:*

> The other shape,
> If shape it might be call'd that shape had none
> Distinguishable in member, joint, or limb,
> Or substance might be call'd that shadow seem'd,
> Fierce as the Furies, terrible as Hell.

Milton describes Satan's horrendous fall in terms of classical mythology, calling the Divinity Jove and Satan Mulciber, Mulciber being a variant name of Vulcan:

> and in Ausonian land
> Men called him Mulciber, and how he fell
> From Heav'n, they fabl'd, thrown by angry Jove
> Sheer o're the Chrystal Battlements: from Morn
> To Noon he fell, from Noon to dewy Eve,
> A summer's day.

So, in Milton, Satan assumes a prestigious role as the protagonist. This concept of the Devil as a heroic figure recurs, particularly in nineteenth-century art and literature. To the nineteenth century he is often an object of reverence, of admiration. The French poet Baudelaire thought that the most perfect type of manly beauty was Milton's Satan. The medieval view, however, still remained traditional. Tasso, the fifteenth-century Italian poet, in his *Gerusalemme Liberata,* depicts him in the horrifying medieval image: shaggy-bearded, red-eyed, foul-breathing, with a mouth slavering with black blood.

Despite the dread that Satan inspires, however, he is sometimes treated, like his attendants, with scant respect. He is turned into a butt, an object of laughter. He is no longer fearsome, no longer effectual. He is himself ensnared by humans, and for an instant the tables are turned. Or his very credulity is his undoing. Such a humorous view of the Fiend was first taken by Dionysius Klein, author of *Tragico-Comoedia,* which was published in 1622. Klein describes a trip to heaven and to hell. Hell is comically equipped with a water tower and other utilities, and the total effect is human risibility and demoniac humiliation. The farcical tone appears later, in *The Ingoldsby Legends* by Richard N. Barham, a nineteenth-century English poet and humorist:

> Old Nick is a black-looking fellow at best,
> Ah, e'en when he's pleased; but never before
> Had he looked so black
> as on seeing his sack
> Thus cut into slits on the Red Sea Shore.

In another of Barham's poetic burlesques, on St. Dunstan and the Devil, the saint gets the better of his enemy by taking his tongs and catching the Evil One by the nose.

In the same vein is *The Devil's Walk,* by Robert Southey, an English contemporary of Barham:

From his brimstone bed, at break of day,
A-walking the Devil is gone,
To look at his snug little farm of the World,
And see how his stock went on.

How then was the Devil dressed?
O, he was in his Sunday's best;
His coat was red, and his breeches were blue,
And there was a hole where his tail came through.

Satan has fallen once more—from the height of the Miltonic conception to the buffoonery represented by such comic images.

In chronicles of medieval days, in occasional ballads and folk sagas and legends, we find a far from heroic Satanic figure. Ingenuity on the part of humans can outwit him, can humiliate him. Once a smith bewitched the devil and put him on an anvil. The devil was so terrified that, when the smith died, he was not admitted to Hell.

A German folk song relates the tale of a highhanded tailor. He comes to Hell for the purpose of clothing the demons. Unexpectedly, however, the tailor ill-treats them all, jabbing them with his scissors and needles. Finally they swear never to let a tailor come near them.

In one legend, a miller ties the Fiend to a water wheel. The villagers of Kleinbautzen, in Germany, where the incident occurred, chuckled long at Satan's discomfiture.

In the case of Martin Luther, the Reformer, the Fiend came quite near him. To Martin Luther, Satan was a reality, a concrete presence, a visual shape. The Great Reformer felt that Satan was actually all around him, provoking, hindering, sneering, attacking. When Luther was engaged in translating the Bible, he observed the Fiend grinning at him. The legend runs that, in a fit of anger, he threw his inkstand at the Devil. "Early this morning," Luther relates, "when I awoke, the Fiend came and began disputing with me. 'Thou art a great sinner,' said he. I replied 'Canst not tell me something new, Satan?' "

Luther believed in incubi and succubi, who have sexual relations with human beings. He believed equally in the aid given to witches and sorcerers by the Satanic legions.

It was, then, no rarity for Satan to be fooled and embarrassed. In *The Devil Is an Ass,* a satirical comedy by Ben Jonson, the play in part attacks witch-hunters and pseudo-demoniacs. The playwright furthermore belittles the Devil's prestige. Human beings become involved in diabolical contrivances. The Great Devil himself, with Pug, the Lesser Devil, discusses the pranks committed by Pug. He can lame a cow. He can enter a sow and make her cast her farrow. Or he can cross a market-woman's mare. But these are trivial accomplishments. He longs to achieve something more meaningful, more effective. Give me a Vice, he appeals to his Master, and I'll show you. So Iniquity appears, joins them as the third member in the Satanic trio. Iniquity enumerates his own activities in gambling and wenching and similar diversions. Our purpose, declares Pug, is to do the Commonwealth of Hell some service. Pug is consequently bidden by his Master to serve the first man he meets. This encounter presents Fitz-Dottrell, Squire of Norfolk. It is a whimsical comedy in which the protagonist is Satan himself, moving and guiding the hapless victims according to his infernal principles. Yet the play itself, by the very wryness of the title, postulates the inane fatuities of the Satanic legend. But then Ben Jonson manifestly transcended popular thought.

Thomas Dekker, also an Elizabethan dramatist, makes Satan, in *The Devil Is in It,* a far from heroic figure. So too in Goethe's version of *Faust,* where Mephistopheles' power is clipped.

In old chronicles, the Devil appears in the Merlin legend. In a political satire on Napoleon III, Victor Hugo presents the Lord playing cards with his Satanic Majesty. Heinrich Heine, in one of his poems, describes an encounter with Satan. Every writer, it appears, every dramatist and poet, every viewer of the complexity of the cosmos and its contents is diverted toward the dark side of thought, the undercurrents of inexplicable activity that somehow impinge on man's awareness that, despite Browning's optimistic cry, all is not right with the world.

But in high dudgeon or not, discomfited and frustrated, Satan can always recapture his sense of power by returning to his lair, his personal domain. Again and again theologians and scholars and demonographers have attempted to locate Satan's Hell with some geographical precision. It has been assigned to Mt. Etna in Sicily. It is on an unknown, remote island everlastingly spouting smoke and flames. St. Brendan, together with his monks, in his adventurous *Voyage,* encountered it in his medieval explorations. Again, with equal assurance, it is situated in the hinterland of the Asian plains. It has entrance gates down to its bottomless depths, and, solely for the use of the fiends themselves, means of egress.

Hell itself is a shadowy realm of gloom, peopled with numberless demons intent on some diabolic operation, preparatory to issuing among gullible men. It has its own peculiar architecture, its specialized fauna, its zones of intense cold alternating with intolerable heat, its wild winds, its beastly animal denizens. At all times, too, it reverberates with the wails and shrieks of ravished souls in torment.

The Church Fathers considered Hell to be situated in the nethermost depths, under the Earth. It was usually regarded as an area partitioned into four sections. The Devil himself sits in one area, resting on the body of Judas Iscariot. Another region is called Purgatory. A third part is assigned to unbaptized infants. In the fourth section dwell the faithful, the devout whose days on earth are ended. Fire and brimstone was no idle allegorical phrase. The Middle Ages accepted the expression in its literal application. In association with the demoniac regions, fire and brimstone became realistic, actual features that were involved in the operations of the Fiend.

Limbus was a term applied to the Jaws of Hell. Limbus was regularly represented by the open maw of a serpentine fiery dragon. From its jaws poured flame, in accordance with the apocalyptic description. Into the midst of the flames are cast the souls of victims who have been entrapped by Satan and his emissaries.

This concept has analogies with Oriental thought. In early Hindu mythology, the name for Hell, the Satanic habitat, was Naglok, snake-land. There was a tribe of Nagas indigenous to the island of Ceylon. The Hindus believed that these Nagas were of reptilian origin, as the term *naga* itself may mean both a native and a snake. In any case, Hell itself was conceived as a sinister, mephitic, snake-ridden haunt.

11

AHRIMAN, SPIRIT OF EVIL

In the ancient Iranian mystic cult of Mithra, life was conceived as a perpetual battle, a conflict between good and evil. The supreme beneficent deity was Ahura Mazda. His colleague was Mithra, the Sun-God. Together, they formed a pair that symbolized a unified duality. Ahura was the image of heaven, and Mithra denoted the celestial light. Mithra became the guardian, the protective agent who maintained a watch, alert and unceasing, over the entire universe. Through his intercession, the Supreme Being destroyed the malefic spirits that conflicted with the inherent goodness in the universe. Furthermore, Mithra imposed his power even upon Ahriman, the Spirit of Darkness.

Ahriman is the Persian Satanic force, the apex in the hierarchy of the somber forces that are in continuous and embattled warfare against Ahura Mazda. The Iranian priests, the Magi who were the repositories of the Mithraic religion in terms of its rituals, its liturgies, and its theological doctrines, conceived Evil as the deified principle that stood in opposition to the Omnipotent Universal Being. But these priests also taught a kind of dualism that required worship of both the Supreme Deity and his adversary, the anti-god, the Genius of Evil. The Supreme Being supported goodness, truth, and light. His enemy was the symbol of falsehood and darkness. The former deity controlled the Yazatas, the kind spirits, while Evil was the commander of a host of malicious demons. These two principles, good and evil, were in constant conflict, the objective being domination over the world: heavenly when the Supreme Being maintains his ascendancy, and infernal when Evil is triumphant.

The votaries of Mithra have a militaristic function. They are unendingly at war with the nether powers. Ethically, the doctrinal conclusion based on this postulate is that man must gather his forces and maintain them at the highest pitch in order to be alert against the assaults of evil, to circumvent these onslaughts, and to obliterate their potential capacities for inflicting every form of catastrophe on mankind. For, exulting in wickedness, in bloody sacrifices, Ahriman's demons bring blight and earthquake and famine. They provoke vile lusts. They stir up sedition and war at the behest of their infernal Master.

Arnobius, the Church Father who flourished early in the fourth century, knew of these evil agents under Ahriman's jurisdiction. The Magi, he declares, consider these anti-gods as spirits of coarse substance who claim divinity and who deceive with their fancies and their falsehoods. Another Church Father, Lactantius (c. 250–c. 317), who was a pupil of Arnobius, asserts that the Master of Evil, the perverted anti-god —whether he is called Satan or Ahriman, is associated with the dark of the night, the atmosphere peculiar to sinister practices. Porphyry, whose life span ran from 232 to around 305 A.D., was a pagan Neoplatonic philosopher, a student of religious cults, who considered that the Egyptian god Sarapis was the counterpart of the Greek Pluto, who in the Mithraic mysteries became Ahriman. Evil was real, Evil was pervasive, and each ancient ethnic community gave it its own national persona, its own conceptual or anthropomorphic form. Plutarch, too, the Greek biographer and philosopher who flourished in the early decades of the second century A.D., calls Ahriman Hades himself, Lord of the Underworld, as the Greeks and Romans conceived him.

Ahriman, who was equated with Hades, and with Pluto, had other attributes as well. Sprung, like Jupiter, from Infinite Time, he dwelt in the tenebrous depths of the Earth. With Hecate, the triple goddess who in her infernal aspect was the deity who presided over the magic arts, Ahriman reigned over the monstrous, unclean forms that were the issue of the mating between Ahriman and the goddess. These pestilential demoniac elementals, the obscene spawn of the Demon of Evil, assaulted high Heaven in an endeavor to overthrow Ahura Mazda. But Evil was crushed then, and hurled down into the darksome abyss. Yet Evil persisted. Ahriman never accepted defeat. And hence, roaming the Earth, bringing in their wake cataclysms and corruption, the mortiferous dwellers in Hell were the portentous messengers of misery, the scourges that created devastation among mankind. Only by expiation, only by supplications and proffered sacrifices, was it possible to appease the demoniac powers. And, in many cases, the initiates in the Mysteries of Mithra could perform certain rituals and pronounce specific incantations that were ruinous to their enemies. Hence Ahriman had two phases, as it were. He was the recognized opponent, as the manifestation of Evil, of the Supremacy of Ahura Mazda. And no less was he an effective ally of men on Earth whose malefic tendencies sought out the nefarious aid of this Spirit. Like the Biblical Satan, then, Ahriman was everlastingly occupied in attempts to impose his maleficent domination upon Heaven and Earth.

The Spirit of Evil, however, in the mysteries of Mithra, is not everlasting. His term of existence is finite. He will be overcome by the Spirit of Good, by the puissant beneficence of Ahura Mazda. When the cosmic time arrives, the horrendous legions controlled by Ahriman will bring destruction upon the world. The universe will then have reached its assigned terminus, its ultimate consummation, just as the ancient Stoics postulated an end to the universe by a cosmic conflagration. In the Mithraic mysteries, a bull of sacred import in the mystic doctrines will appear. Mithra will arise. Man will be resurrected. The graves will give forth the dead. The newly reawakened mortals will retain their former appearance, and there will be a universal recognition. Then the Supreme Being will bring down a conflagration upon the Earth. The wicked will perish. Ahriman and his obscene satellites will be destroyed along with their foul master. Unalloyed happiness, free from evil, from the threats and machinations of Ahriman, will achieve its ultimate, infinite purpose.

III

DEMONIAC SATELLITES

SATAN, THE Archfiend, does not stand alone. He has a vast, militaristic organization, consisting of subsidiary echelons of powers. These fiends can assume innumerable forms, animal and human, invisible and tangible. One medieval miracle play alludes to their appearance and their temperaments: They are horned, sometimes hairy, playful, foolish, male and female, youthful or aged, incubi and succubi, formed from the rays of planets, from human sperm, from human odors. They may take the shape of satyrs and fauns, trulls, or nymphs. They may haunt lakes or perch on mountain tops, or secrete themselves in the fastnesses of dense forests, or in regions uninhabited by man. In substance they vary. They are igneous and earthy. They are formed of cloudy exhalations, or compounded of animal carcasses.

In the ancient cults of Chaldea, they were frequently represented as human in body, crowned with a lion's head, and with the feet of an eagle. Sometimes they took on a dog shape, lion-clawed, with a scorpion's tail, goat horns, a skeletal head, and four outstretched wings—a composite picture of characteristics straight from Hell. Goya, the eighteenth-

34

century Spanish painter, often represented Satan in one or more of these horrendous forms, imaginatively fearsome, yet retaining elements of tremendous realism.

John Weirus, a sixteenth-century demonographer, conceived the demoniac hierarchy as composed of these ranks:

One emperor
Seven kings
Twenty-four dukes
Thirteen demons with the title of marquis
Ten counts
Eleven presidents

This hierarchy was determined by the degree of wickedness of the demons. Those winged demons, who can be everywhere at the same instant, are ranked as powers, principalities, rulers of the darkness. There are spirits of sheer malevolence and unclean creatures who, themselves banished from heaven, seek to destroy. They terrify the imagination. They contrive blasphemies by concealing themselves in temples. They blight crops. They assist necromancers in their ghostly machinations.

Just as Heaven, the seas, and Hades were assigned respectively to Zeus, Poseidon, and Pluto in classical mythology, so in the Satanic realm Oriens ruled the spirits of the East, while the West was under the jurisdiction of Boul. To Amemon fell the supervision of the South, and the regions of the North were assigned to Eltzen.

In the sixteenth century, a German demonographer named Sigmund Feyerabend produced a monumental and encyclopedic *Theatrum Diabolorum*. It contains essays on the existence of demons, their nature and functions and powers. Among the contributors to the volume were Ludovicus Milichius, Andreas Fabricius Chemnicensis, and Hermannus Hamelmannus. They were all versed in occult matters. The total number of demons, according to the estimate recorded in Chapter 8, reaches 2,665,866,746,664. Special types of demons are described in detail. These include the Devil of Blasphemy, the Dance-Devil, the Hunting-Devil, the Wedlock-Devil, the Devil of Tyranny, the Devil of Unchastity, the Devil of Laziness, the Devil of Pride, the Devil of Gambling, the Servants' Devil, the Devil of Pestilence.

Jacob Ruffs dramatized the story of Job and the parable of the vineyard. The latter was performed at Zürich in 1539. In the play, Satan sows seeds of sedition and induces the servants of the vineyard to slay their master.

But Satan's satellites are no less destructive than their Lord. One grimoire, highly popular in the Middle Ages, was *The Key of Solomon*. This magic manual classifies the Satanic hierarchy in another form, adding specific names, order of priority, and functions of demons. The Emperor is Lucifer, the Bearer of Light. His Prime Minister is Beelzebub, and his Grand Duke is Astorath. There follows a series of names to which are attached military designations and ranks, as Grand Generals Satanachia and Agaliarept, a Lieutenant General named Fleuretty, Brigadier Sargatanas, and Field Marshal Nebiros. Below these ranks are secondary spirits: Marbas and Guseyn, Botis, Abigar and Valefar, Nuberus, Pursan, Pruslas, Foräu, Bathim, Ayperos, Loray, Clasyabolas, Belphegor, bearded, with phallic tongue and drooling mouth. Other hordes are slaves of the higher echelons. In order to invoke their cooperation, the precise ritual must be performed with minute exactitude. If this is done, the spirits will be subservient to the mighty sovereignty of Satan himself and will disclose hidden treasures, confer invisibility, reveal the great mysteries of the universe, and exorcise the spirits of the dead.

Porphyry, the Greek Neoplatonist, mentions several types of demons. According to popular opinion, he adds, these nameless beings, associated with dark cults, are roused to anger if neglected. If they receive no regular veneration, they become actively hostile. But, if appeased by supplication, their favor may be enlisted, under the aegis of Caaerinolaas, the Grand President of Hell. On the other hand, the ways of Satan are of such a nature that any known practice of his was shunned or negated by human beings. Whatever was Satanic was suspect. In Turkish legend, only the first three fingers were used in eating, for the belief was that Satan used the two other fingers for that purpose.

The functions of Satan's henchmen are as variable as they are multiple. Some of the fiends are teachers of crafts to human beings. They instruct also in enchantments. They expound astrological lore. Some again are herbalists and are skilled in the virtues and properties of plants. Nor are all of them confined to the territory of Hell. They ascend to the upper Earth.

Peter Lombard, who spans the twelfth century, was among the most eminent personalities of his time. He was the Master of Sentences, the great Scholastic. Yet at great length and with the utmost sobriety, he discusses the nature and habits of demons. In his acceptance of Satan's attendants, he is followed a century later by Albertus Magnus, philosopher and scientist.

Some spirits are called elementals. They are associated with the four cosmic elements: fire, air, earth, water. Other elementals have their habitat underground, shunning the light of day. In character they are represented as fierce and malicious. They cause shipwrecks upon the seas. They create storms. They indulge in earthquakes. Lonely travelers are killed and torn apart by them. Yet, like human beings, they sometimes show kindly ways and even refrain from unending destruction.

The more important demons subservient to the Archfiend himself have their special functions, their particular province of action. In Hell they administer justice. Like the ancient Radamanthus, they mete out punishments to guilty sinners.

Or they may function as commanders-in-chief of vast demoniac legionary troops. Some even rise to divine sovereignty, to godhead among the pagan nations of Asia Minor. Thus Baal, Moloch, Milcom, Baalberith, Nergal, Dagon, Rimmon, and Chamas were all originally infernal princes in the nether hierarchy.

Some demons live in the ocean depths. Others have their abode in the circumambient air. Still others haunt the dark woods and forests, forbidding precipices, desert wastes. At the time of the Sabbat gatherings they appear in Thuringia and Westphalia, at the Spirato della Mirandola in Italy, on the Babia Gora in the Carpathians, the Old Women's Mountain. From their habitations they stream to the ends of the Earth, for distance has no meaning for them.

They are said to possess knowledge in every field, but not equally in the same degree. Some are inconceivably cunning. Yet there are dullards and robots too among them, stupid and insensate, just barely capable of following orders, never of initiating an enterprise. They understand the natural phenomena—storms and convulsions and floods. They are conversant with the sacred Biblical writings, which they can quote appositely and perversely. They know man's evil thoughts and schemes. They can estimate events from astrological calculations. Whatever they do, they do under strict commands. They have the ability to course through the four elements—fire, air, earth, water—with phenomenal speed, through all the confines of the Universe. In short, in their cumulative capacities, according to their individual functions and their peculiar attributes, they have dominion over the cosmos.

In Biblical and Rabbinical literature, evil spirits are designated in a variety of ways. They are *shedim,* and *mazzikim,* injurers; *ruah,* an evil spirit; *mal'ache satan,* messengers of Satan; *mal'ache habalah,* messengers of destruction.

In Kabalistic literature, *kelifoth*—shells—are supernatural powers that affect man's existence and his conduct, as well as natural phenomena.

The *shed* was always a malevolent spirit in Jewish folklore. But in ancient Babylonia, the *shed* was usually a benevolent and protective spirit.

Another group of spirits in Biblical literature consisted of *se'irim*—hairy, goat-shaped forms like satyrs, malignant and hostile to the Divinity.

In general, Rabbinical writings are packed with allusions to demons, their names and nature, their functions and activities, together with directions on how to avoid or overcome them.

Among the revolting activities of Satan's servitors is their habit of copulating with human beings. The union produces offspring called cambions. The fiends copulate with each other as well. But most often they would rather, as incubi, press their defiling attentions on women. They could fecundate them by obscene transference of seminal fluid from male humans to women. They could propagate and beget. In the medieval chronicles, many a woman was known to have felt fiendish embraces and to have undergone diabolic intercourse. Sometimes the victim died from sheer fright. Sometimes she remained silent, while her simple, unsuspecting husband went his way. On occasion, women were prepared to continue some fiendish *affaire* for years. Housewives were often such connubial partners. Nuns would be forced into demoniac intimacy. But in the case of a witch, there was no reluctance to become a Satanic mistress. In the folklore of Central Europe, Satan himself was quite domesticated in this regard. He was credited, too, with a grandmother and, naturally or not, with a devilish mother. And when Satan himself fell in love, he did so with diabolic passion. Lermontov's poem *The Demon* sets the Fiend in the bleak desolation of the Caucasus, where Prometheus was once fettered and confined. There Satan becomes passionately enamored of the beautiful Tamara.

In medieval history, *the offspring of the Devil* was an expression used of the barbaric Huns. Again, children born with deformed figures—crippled, hydrocephalic, or unbalanced in any sense—were believed to be the Devil's spawn and were not suffered to live. Cain was thus believed to be the issue of Eve and an incubus, while Attila the Gothic king and the Emperor Theodoric were both taken to be Satan's sons. The infamous tyrant of Padua, Ezzelino da Romano, was likewise allegedly a Satanic offspring. In these cases, it is evident that the attribution of a Satanic paternity is due to the bestial character of the offspring.

The total number of demons was discussed and estimated by Hugo of St. Victor, the twelfth-century Scholastic philosopher, by St. Thomas Aquinas, by Rabbis, by St. Chrysostom, and others. Some estimated the total to reach billions. Mystic Kabalistic calculations recorded that Satan's satellites numbered exactly 7,405,926. The apocryphal *Book of Enoch the Patriarch,* ascribed to the second century B.C., contains a great deal of demonological matter—items on the number of Satanic hosts, and on the infernal hierarchy. Other investigations were concerned with the corporeal composition of demons, with their subtilized nature. Isidore of Seville, a medieval encyclopedist, said that demons had bodies constituted of air. Others asserted that they ate smoke rising from burning corpses: also blood, fire, and flies. Some demons, endowed with human characteristics, even fell sick, or died.

Among the functions of the devils are their ingenious punitive operations. They note down sins and crimes committed furtively. They keep a record of devotions that are merely lip service. They maintain a watchful eye on lechery practiced among lustful clerics. They flog and strangle women who are too lavish in dress or who beautify their faces to allure weak men. They drag such women off to Hell. With hooks and hatchets they tear and chop and flay the dead and the living. They tear out souls and hammer them on anvils. They torment with fire and flame, alternating with biting, searing cold.

In Indian demonology there are lustful incubi and succubi, who make coitus with humans their primary function. They are known as bhutums and churels respectively.

Every country has its own national and ethnic demonology. Gnomids, for instance, dwell in the Earth, and kostchtchie are Russian demons whose habitat is the Caucasus. Leshy are Slavic rustic creatures. Spain has duendes, who are incubi. In Tibet a demon may be created by merely thinking with concentration. Such thought-forms of demons are known as egrigors.

A vivid evocation of a Satanic spectacle appears in Benvenuto Cellini's *Autobiography*. Cellini (1500–1571) was a distinguished Italian sculptor and goldsmith and, as was not unusual in the Renaissance, was deeply involved in the occult. The setting of his account is the Colosseum in Rome, at midnight:

Through certain odd circumstances it came about that I gained the friendship of a Silician priest, a man of most lofty mind, and with an excellent knowledge of Latin and Greek. While we were conversing one day together, we chanced to talk of the art of necromancy, concerning which I said, "All my life long I have had the greatest desire to see and hear something of it." Whereupon the priest answered, "Strong and steady must be the mind of him who sets himself to such an enterprise." I replied that strength and steadiness of mind I should have and to spare, if only I had the means of testing these. Then answered the priest, "If you have but the courage for it, I'll give you your fill of the rest." So we agreed to put the thing in hand. One evening the priest began to make his preparations, and told me I was to find a companion or two, but not more. I called on my great friend Vincenzio Romoli, and he brought with him a Pistoja man, who was also given to necromancy. Together we set off for the Coliseum, and there, having dressed himself after the wont of magicians, the priest began to draw circles on the ground, with the finest rites and ceremonies you can imagine. Now he had bidden us bring precious perfumes and fire, and evil-smelling stuff as well. When all was ready, he made an entrance to the circle, and, taking us by the hand, led us one by one within. Then he distributed the duties. The pentacle he gave into the hands of his companion magician; we others were given the care of the fire for the perfumes; and he began his conjuring. This had lasted more than an hour and a half, when there appeared many legions of spirits, so that the Coliseum was full of them. I was attending to the precious incense, and when the priest perceived the great multitudes, he turned to me and said, "Benvenuto, ask of them something." I answered, "Let them transport me to my Sicilian Angelica." That night he got no reply at all, but my eager interest in the thing was satisfaction enough for me. The necromancer told us we must come back another time, when I should have the fulfillment of my desire. But he wished me to bring with me a young boy of perfect purity.

So I brought a shop-boy of mine about twelve years old. Once more I sent for Vincenzio Romoli; and as a certain Agnolino Gaddi was a close friend of both of us, we took him too on the business. When we had again reached the appointed place, the necromancer made the same preparation with even greater care, and led us into the circle, which he made this time with still more wonderful skill and ceremonies. Then he gave to my friend Vincenzio the care of the perfumes and the fire, with Agnolino Gaddi to help him, put the pentacle into my hand, telling me to turn it in the direction he would indicate, while under the pentacle stood my little shop-boy. This done, the necromancer began to utter the most terrible invocations, and to call by their names many of the princes of the demoniac legions (speaking the while in Hebrew words, also in Greek and Latin), and commanding them, by the strength and power of God increate, living, and eternal; so that in a brief space the whole

Coliseum was full of them, and there were a hundred times more than there had been the first night. Meanwhile Vincenzio Romoli, along with Agnolino, was attending to the fire and to the burning of the precious perfumes. Once more I asked, by advice of the magician, to be with Angelica. Then he turned to me and said, "Do you hear what they say? — that in a month's time you will be where she is." And again he entreated me to stand firm, for the legions were a thousand more than he had called; and since they had agreed to what I had asked, we must speak soft to them, and gently bid them go. On the other side, the boy, who was under the pentacle, said, all trembling, that round us were a million of the most warlike men, and that they were threatening us. Moreover, said he, four huge giants had appeared. They were armed, and they made as if they would enter our circle. At this the necromancer, who was shaking with fright, tried with all the soft and gentle words he could think of to bid them go. Vincenzio Romoli, looking after the perfumes, was quivering like a reed. But I, who was just as much afraid, forced on myself a braver mien, and inspirited them in wonderful fashion, though, indeed, I nearly died when I saw the magician's fright. The boy, who had put his head between his knees, said, "I'll die in this way, since die we must." Then I said to the child, "These creatures are all lower than us, and what you see is only smoke and shade; so lift your eyes." When he had done so he spoke once more, "The whole Coliseum is on fire, and the fire is upon us"; and, putting his hand to his face, again he said he was dead, and he would not look any more. The necromancer entreated me to stand by him, also to make fumes of assafoetida. So, turning to Vincenzio Romoli, I told him to do this, and looked at Agnolino Gaddi the while, whose eyes were starting from his head with terror, and who was more than half dead. "Agnolo," I said to him, "this is no time to shiver and shake. Up and make yourself useful! Throw the assafoetida quickly on the fire." At the instant when he moved to do this, he yielded so powerfully to the needs of nature that it served better than the assafoetida. The boy lifted his head at this great stench and noise, and, hearing me laugh, his fear was calmed a little, and he told us the spirits were riding off tumultuously. So

we remained till the chimes of day began to sound. Then again
the boy spoke, saying that but few remained, and they were far
off. The magician, having gone through the rest of his ceremonies, doffed his robes, gathered up a great load of books he had
brought, and we all came out of the circle together, sticking as
close as possible to one another—especially the boy, who squeezed
himself into the middle of us, and clutched the magician by the
vest and me by the cloak. On our way towards our houses in the
Banks, he told us that two of the demons he had seen in the
Coliseum were going before us, now leaping, now running over
the roofs, now along the ground. The wizard told us that in all
the times he had entered the circles nothing so great had ever
happened to him. And he tried to persuade me to help him in
making incantations over a book. Out of this we should draw
infinite riches; for we should ask the demons to teach us where
to find the treasures, of which the earth was full, and thus
should become very rich. As for love and such-like things, he
said they were vanity and folly, which profited nothing at all. I
answered that if I were learned in Latin I would do so right
willingly. But he persuaded me that Latin letters would in no
wise serve me; that, had he wished, he could have got many a
one learned in Latin; but that he had never found any man of
so steadfast a mind, and that I should give heed to his counsel.
Talking thus, we reached our homes, and all that night each of
us dreamt of devils.

Among their other bestialities, demons condemn humans
to the stake. They boil and roast bodies in cauldrons. They
hang them from trees. But in all these functions they require
assistance. They use the help of monstrous creatures of in-
describable ferocity and repulsiveness. They devour human
skin. They make dishes out of the bodies of every type of
sinner, from thieves to harlots, from monks to sodomites.
And these dishes are served up as a huge infernal cannibal-
istic banquet, in the style of the Marquis de Sade's *Le Petit
Fils d'Hercule*.

The demons had their own fears too. They were not exempt from concern for their individual nature. They could be diverted or terrified or driven into flight. Holiness of an anchorite could bewilder them into inaction. Or passionately devout prayers. Or hymns. Or the sign of the cross. Even some plants and herbs, particularly garlic, were considered efficacious in resisting their approaches.

If a holy man spat on Satan, the latter, crushed, fled in defeat. One saint bound him ignominiously in fetters. Another lured him into a cave where he imprisoned the Fiend. Still another belabored Satan with a heavy cudgel. The Devil may be caught in a goblet or other receptacle and held fast, a restless but helpless captive. For, in the course of the confrontations between the Evil One and his prospective victims, he is not always the victor. A staunch and fearless anchorite or an equally devout nun may circumvent his snares. For a brief instant, in fact, Satan may be caught redhanded and convicted like any human criminal. In a fifteenth-century *Processus Luciferi*, Satan is actually brought to trial, prosecuted, and condemned.

In sympathy with their Master, the demons wander over the Earth in their defiling abandonment. They solace themselves by destroying human beings. Attaching themselves to particular persons, they secretly work into the very vitals, ruining health, spreading disease, terrorizing the mind with feverish dreams and hallucinations. They seek to arouse and maintain hatreds among men, with resultant economic and political and military upheavals. It is never man who creates havoc and chaos in the universe. It is always the work of the fiendish agents. But there are some remedies at hand—some form of confrontation, if not of final victory, over these forces. For apotropaic purposes, to deter these spirits and avert their stratagems, one may use fire as a powerful protective agent: also water, or light, or bread, salt, or herbs. One such herb in particular, called parmanable, was reputed to possess specific virtues. If one carried the root of the herb on one's person, it was possible to drive off the devil or even make him do one's bidding.

Yet the demons seem to be repeatedly successful in their assaults. For they themselves possess human passions and emotions. King Solomon, relates the *Koran,* enlisted their aid in achieving his supernatural enterprises. He selected demons who were expert builders. Others he found to be adept at pearl-diving. And under the King's power, they assumed the attitudes of human workers, and their very tasks which they accomplished were a measure of their success.

Josephus the historian stresses the close association between King Solomon and his shadowy servitors. They taught him necromancy, and his reputation for thaumaturgic performances was universally known from Ethiopia to Persia, from the Black Sea to the coast of China. He had become, thanks to the unusual cooperation of the infernal creatures, a global personality, the Arch Magician, the Performer of Miraculous Deeds. With the additional support of gnomes and undines, elves and salamanders, he became Lord of the Occult Arts, endowed with supreme power, like the later Dr. Faustus, by his involvement with the Master of the Demons. Periapts and invocations, amulets, pentacles, charms of all types were so much the more efficacious when linked with the Solomonic legend. Solomon's Lamp had the virtue of Aladdin's lamp. Solomon's Mirror, the Seal of Solomon, the Ring of Solomon studded with magic stones, the Magic Carpet of Solomon— all these objects constituted the demoniac apparatus that enslaved the fiends to one's will. In the Middle Ages, manuals on witchcraft, entitled grimoires, were current as the writings of Solomon himself and were considered the final word in thaumaturgic practices. *The Testament of Solomon, The Lesser Key of Solomon, The Clavicle of Solomon* were seriously studied and consulted as late as the seventeenth century by scholars and physicians and other earnest students and practitioners of the occult.

IV

THE SATANIC PACT

MAN HAS invariably striven to cross the frontiers of human achievement. Driven by boundless ambition, free of all restraints, man has lusted after imperial or military authority, after wealth and luxury, after power over foreign peoples, sensuous and desirable conquests of women, long life, endless life. He has craved for knowledge of the arcane secrets of alchemy and the mysteries of nature. And in the heat of these passions, man has been ready to pay the cost.

With his acknowledged shrewd judgment of human weaknesses, Satan has come forward to offer generous but binding conditions, abundance of the rich prizes of this Earth, in exchange for man's eternal soul.

Thus the concept of a Satanic pact grew in men's minds, from an indeterminate but naggingly persistent longing and hope into a tremendous actuality. In saga and myth, in drama and folk ballad, the Satanic Pact became a theme capable of endless variations. Every pact brought fulfillment and achievement, and the question of repayment was after all a man's own concern. Thus, by gradual steps, the idea took on a strong possibility, a reality. The imaginative myth, born of vague human desires and yearnings, became the logos, and the logos, the word, became the deed, the act.

There are pertinent records and testimonies among the lives of the early saints and chroniclers. Certain men, in some convulsive frenzy, made the infernal contract, giving their blood bond. There was Theophilus, who looked after a church in Cilicia, in Asia Minor. When the new Abbot dismissed him from his position, Theophilus suddenly turned ambitious. He longed for greater honors, a more dignified status. In the event, he renounced Christianity and allied himself with Satan. But his acquisitions became empty and meaningless to him. In a fit of contrition he began to fast and pray, and finally he was absolved. But he had made the Pact, and Satan had virtually won his soul.

Some of the Popes were believed to have had similar demoniac negotiations—notably Sylvester II, Benedict IX, and Gregory VII.

A human being may summon Satan for his own purpose, but in that case he will be bound by an ineluctable pact. The pact is often concluded and confirmed by the signature of the suppliant, in his own blood. But the agreement may be consummated, as in the drama of Dr. Faustus, by calling upon the Fiend with a certain magic formula. One summons ran as follows:

Palas aron azinomas.

Sometimes the words used are Hebraic, or Latin, or Aramaic, or Greek, and on occasion they are a mixture of several languages, together with expressions that have no known connotation. Another mystic utterance is again formulaic:

Bagahi laca Bachabé.

These invocations are merely the last step in the Satanic ritual. This ritual includes the drawing of the five-pointed figure called the pentacle, the proper clothing to be worn, the careful position of the body during sleep on the previous night, and the selection of an appropriate spot for the final utterance. If the suppliant changes his mind and wishes to break the pact, he must steal the signed document himself. This is an act fraught with terrifying hazards to body and soul. Some of those who fell under Satan's control did break the agreement, but with infinite agony.

There are medieval instances of circumventing the Satanic conditions of the pact. This requires deep subtlety, and also the enlistment of religious, Christian aid. The German ballad of St. Gertrude illustrates this situation. A knight met the Devil in a dark forest and was offered untold treasure in exchange for his lady love. The knight brought the Devil to a chapel, but, instead of the promised maid, the Queen of Heaven herself appeared, and the Devil was routed.

In this connection, there is a medieval German formula for renouncing Satan and his demons:

QUESTION: Forsakest thou the Devil?
ANSWER: I forsake the Devil.
Q.: And all Devil guilds?
A.: And I forsake all Devil guilds.
Q.: And all Devil works?
A.: And I forsake all Devil works, and words, Thonar and Wodan and Saxnot and all the evil ones that are his companions.

When the Devil is invoked and there is a Satanic response, a sudden blast of cold air chills the suppliant. A misty shape appears, forming into something ghastly and spectral. Then the sorcerer or witch or necromancer enters into an agreement or pact. A *pactum expressum* is an arrangement executed by signs or spoken words or in writing. A *pactum tacitum*, a silent negotiation, merely seeks Satanic aid.

The pact is written on virgin parchment. The idea of newness was peculiar to magic rites. Fresh or new objects of all types, such as plants, utensils, virgin soil, unused parchment, were among the sorcerer's required stock in trade. The suppliant signs with his own blood. The minute conditions affecting the pact are recorded in a treatise entitled *Compendium Maleficarum,* The Witches' Manual. The author is a seventeenth-century demonographer named Francesco Maria Guazzo.

One demonographer said that the Devil himself wrote the contract with the Magician's blood. The conditions of the covenant generally involved the signer's soul after his death, or after a specified time (as a rule twenty years). *Isaiah* 28:15 suggests such a pact:

We have made a covenant with death and with hell are we in agreement.

In the fifth century, the Church Father Origen appeared to confirm the possibility of such an agreement.

At various trials in the course of the seventeenth century, witches would offer the court the contracts that they had confessedly made with the Devil. A notorious magician, Urbain Grandier, who was executed in 1634, made a pact that is preserved in the Bibliothèque Nationale in Paris. Grandier was accused by the Ursuline nuns of Loudun of practicing bewitchment. At his trial the devils who spoke out of the mouths of the obsessed nuns were called as witnesses. In further evidence against Grandier, two documents were produced. One was the pact between Grandier and Satan: It was signed by Grandier himself. The other document was signed by six devils, the signatures being authenticated, in mirror writing, by Baalbarith, Satan's Secretary.

Another demoniac covenant has likewise been preserved. It concerns Father Louys Gaufridy, who in 1611 was strangled and then burned at Aix-en-Provence for bewitching and seducing two nuns. At his trial he confessed that, as a min-

ister of Satan, he had performed the Black Mass. The pledge
to his diabolic master ran as follows:

> I, Louys Gaufridy,
> give my body and soul to Lucifer
> before whom I stand . . .
> and thus do I sign to witness it.

One type of procedure relating to a pact is known from
accounts preserved in medieval grimoires. At sunrise the suppliant cuts with a new knife a branch of wild hazel. This
he carries to a deserted spot, near some crumbling castle, an
empty house, or a disused hut. With a bloodstone, he forms
a triangle on the floor and sets two wax candles nearby. The
pact has to be written within the circle drawn around the
triangle. Otherwise the covenant is nullified. Within the circle the karcist, standing with the hazel wand in his hand,
first pronounces the nine mystic names, as *The Key of Solomon* recommends:

> *El*
> *Iod*
> *Eheieh*
> *Tetragrammaton Elohim*
> *Eloah va—Daath*
> *Elohim Gibor*
> *El Adonai Tzabaoth*
> *Elohim Tzabaoth*
> *Shaddai*

Then he utters the dread conjuration:

> Obey promptly, or you will be
> tortured eternally. So come
> forth by the force of these
> potent words—*Aglon*
> *Tetragram Vaycheon*

Stimulammathon
Meffias Soter Emmanuel
Sabaoth Adonai!
Te adoro et invoco!
I worship you and invoke you!

Or the spirit may be summoned by the following command, pronounced thrice:

I conjure you, O spirit,
to appear by the power of Great Adonai,
by Eloim, by Ariel, Johavam, Agla,
Tagla, Mathon.

One must address the Fiend thus:

Emperor Lucifer, Master of all the rebellious spirits, I beg you to be favorable in the invocation that I make to your great Minister Lucifuge Rofocale, as I wish to make a pact with him.

O Count Astorah! Be propitious, and bring it to pass that, this very night, the great Lucifuge appear to me in human form, and that he grant me, by means of the pact that I shall offer him, all the wealth that I need.

O great Lucifuge! I beg you to leave your abode . . . Obey promptly, or you will be tortured eternally by the force of the potent words of the Great Key of Solomon.

Christopher Marlowe, the Elizabethan dramatist, offers another invocation in his *Tragical History of Doctor Faustus:*

May the gods of Acheron be propitious to me. May the triple power of Iehoua avail me. Hail, spirits of fire and water, Beelzebub, Prince of the East, Monarch of the burning Lower Regions, and demigorgon. Be propitious, that Mephistopheles may appear and arise. Why do you delay? By Iehoua, by Gehenna and the consecrated water that I now sprinkle, and the sign of the cross that I now make, and by our vows, let the said Mephistopheles himself now arise in our presence.

In early necromantic rites that involved the evocation of the spirits of the dead, these spirits were addressed as *'elohim.* Later, however, the term *'elohim* designated solely the Supreme Being.

V

SATAN IN THE MIDDLE AGES

IN MEDIEVAL literature, Satan achieves his avatar. He appears in innumerable disguises: bestial, human, and insubstantial. Anecdotes, memoirs, hagiographies, chronicles of various kinds all testify, with documentary evidence, to his presence on Earth and his practices. In the mystery and morality plays that were a popular form of both entertainment and religious instruction, Satan is the primary adversary, the arch enemy of every pious act. He is the deceiver of men. He overshadows the entire spiritual life of the Middle Ages. No one, saint or sinner, serf or baron, is free from his guile, from the terror of his ruthless presence, his implacable aggression. On the stage he was readily identified by his limp, the result of his fall from Heaven.

In the *Mystery of St. Desiderius,* Satan and his bodyguards appear. They are thrashed, ridiculed, bound in fetters. In another play, Satan himself is thrashed by his own fiends. These religious dramas were performed regularly in many countries—in France, England, Germany, Italy. They reflect the common attitude, compounded of dread and contempt, toward the Satanic concept.

On the other hand, in a seventeenth-century Spanish comedy, *El Diablo Predicador,* Satan is represented as a preacher. Demons, in fact, often made pretensions of being devout Christians, chanting hymns and psalms, and professing the orthodox faith.

Satan is constantly at pains to subvert innocence, to debauch saintliness, to seduce chastity. He is perpetually (and usually ineffectively) wrestling with hermits in the Thebaid, in their cells, at prayer. During their vigils and their dreams, he presents himself in the enticing form of a beautiful, voluptuous woman. When Satan's efforts seem futile, in his frenzied rage he foams and splutters and resumes one of his bestial shapes: goat-headed, horned, covered with coarse, matted hair, cloven-hoofed. In his frustration, he belches sulphurous fumes, lashing his shaggy tail, then disappearing, *sfumato,* in mistiness.

Young girls and devout matrons are particularly exposed to his wiles. He diverts boys from their studies, from their devotions, and from their affection for their parents. He also plays pranks, at times whimsical, sometimes less innocuous. Not infrequently his triumphs are short-lived, and he vanishes to his invisible domain, disappointed, cursing and damning, in a whorl of acrid smoke.

St. Bernard of Clairvaux, the famous twelfth-century churchman, listed the numerous devices employed by Satan to tempt men and women.

The *Chronicle* of Salimbene (1221–1288), an Italian monk, gives an account of Satan's guile in his frequent change of form. A friar, relates Salimbene, often encountered Satan: once in the likeness of St. Francis, again as St. Clare, then in the images of St. Anthony and St. Agnes, and lastly as Christ Himself.

In a thirteenth-century Regula, or body of rules for hermits, considered to be the work of a canon of the Augustinian order, advice is given on how the recluse should conduct himself when tempted by the Devil:

Every night the recluse should keep a lamp burning, at least when he completes the services of the nocturnal hours. Let him disregard dreams utterly, if a vision bids him do something very pious and rebukes him for his concern on some point or other. For the Devil is wont to tempt the sleeper to perform good deeds, so that, when he does so, he may confound those who have kept vigil. Now every single person should know that the Devil, on account of his cunning nature, can foresee certain future events. If a recluse does not perform the good works about which he is advised in his dreams, his soul may incur damnation. For this reason, in this nocturnal vision the Devil changes into an angel of light, and presently, during vigils, destroys the soul of the innocent victim. Also, the Enemy usually advises the weak, in a night vision, to obtain either a blessing or a prayer or food from the recluse and thus become pious themselves. The versatile Devil operates in this way to drag souls into the vice of pride, if the recluse's indiscretion thinks that it is done for his benefit. No one can enumerate the wiles of the Enemy. Hence one must be careful if he has to live without a teacher or a guide and if he wants to resist the Devil's stratagems.

St. Godric of Finchale, a medieval monk, was tempted by the Devil to work beyond his strength so that he would be compelled to abandon his saintly career:

When St. Godric, tired out by his labor, was taking a rest, a stranger who stood by, observing him for a time, spoke thus: "Surely the Fathers of days gone by, whom you admit that you imitate, did not labor in the desert, hungry and pale. Look, from morning to noon you have dug up scarcely ten feet of earth, although you ought to show your spiritual devotion to God by the extent of your labor."

In reply the man of God said smilingly: "Show me then an example of good work by digging first."

He thought that the stranger was a good man, sent by God to teach him. So, handing over his spade, St. Godric said: "The time for the usual prayer compels me to return to the oratory. When I come back I shall listen to you, and I shall gladly accept what you rightly advise me."

The stranger quickly seized hold of the spade and began to turn the earth energetically.

When Godric came back, he found that more work had been done than he usually finished in eight days. Then the stranger said: "This is the way you too ought to have followed the example of the Fathers, with the constant sweat of your brow."

At sight of this, the holy man gave a shudder, for he realized that this was not a real man. He was, in fact, quite dark and hairy, tall in stature; and for all his labor in digging there appeared no sign whatever of toil and sweat.

Godric returned to his cell and came back with a book he had put into his cassock.

"Tell me," he said, "who you are and why you have come here."

The other answered: "Don't you see that I am a man like yourself?"

"If you are a man," retorted Godric, "tell me whether you believe in the Father and the Son and the Holy Ghost and worship the mother of the Lord with me."

The stranger said: "Do not worry about my belief: this questioning is no concern of yours."

Approaching him, Godric took out his book containing the pictures of the Savior and holy Mary and St. John, and quickly thrust it into the other's face. "See," he said, "if you believe in God, kiss these pictures reverently." But the other, unable to endure it any longer, spat on the book and vanished derisively. The ground that the stranger had dug up Godric left untilled for seven years, but after that he sprinkled holy water over it and at the end of the seventh year he tilled it.

Another tale dealing with the Devil's wiles in trying to ensnare a recluse runs as follows:

There formerly lived a hermit, who in a remote cave passed night and day in the service of God. At no great distance from his cell a shepherd tended his flock. It happened that this person one day fell into a deep sleep, and in the meantime a robber, perceiving his carelessness, carried off his sheep. When the keeper awoke and discovered the theft, he began to swear in good set terms that he had lost his sheep; and where they were conveyed was totally beyond his knowledge. Now, the lord of the flock, when he heard this, was filled with rage and commanded him to be put to death. This gave great umbrage to the hermit before mentioned. "O Heaven," said he to himself, "seest thou this deed? The innocent suffers for the guilty; why permittest thou such things? If thus injustice triumph, why do I remain here? I will again enter the world, and do as other men do."

With these feelings, he quitted his hermitage and returned into the world; but God willed not that he should be lost; an angel in the form of a man was commissioned to join him. Accordingly, crossing the hermit's path, he thus accosted him: "My friend, where are you going?"

"I go," said the other, "to the city before us."

"I will accompany you," replied the angel. "I am a messenger from heaven, and come to be the associate of your way."

They walked on together toward the city. When they had entered, they entreated for the love of God harborage during the night at the house of a certain knight, who received them with cheerfulness and entertained them with much magnificence. The knight had an only son lying in the cradle, whom he exceedingly loved. After supper, their bedchamber was sumptuously decorated; and the angel retired with the hermit to rest. But about the middle of the night the angel got up and strangled the sleeping infant. The hermit, horror-struck at what he had witnessed, said within himself, "Never can this be an angel of God. The good knight gave him everything that was necessary; he had but this poor innocent, and this strange companion of mine has strangled him." Yet he was afraid to reprove him.

In the morning both arose and went forward to another city, in which they were honorably entertained at the house of one of the inhabitants. This person possessed a superb golden cup which he highly valued; and which, during the night, the angel pur-loined. The hermit thought, "Verily, this is one of the lost an-gels; our host has treated us well, and yet he has robbed him." But still he held his peace, for his apprehension was extreme.

On the morrow they continued their journey; and as they walked they came to a certain river, over which a bridge was thrown; they ascended the bridge, and about midway a poor man met them.

"My friend," said the angel to him, "show us the way to yon-der city."

The pilgrim turned and pointed with his finger to the road they were to take; but, as he turned, the angel seized him by the shoulders and precipitated him into the stream below. At this the terrors of the hermit were again aroused—"It is the Devil," exclaimed he internally, "it is the Devil, and no good angel! What evil had the poor man done that he should be drowned?"

He would now have departed alone; but was afraid to give utterance to the thoughts of his heart.

About the hour of vespers they reached a city in which they again sought shelter for the night; but the master of the house to whom they applied sharply refused it.

"For the love of Heaven," said the angel, "afford us a shelter, lest we fall a prey to the wolves and other wild beasts." The man pointed to a sty—"That," said he, "is inhabited by pigs; if it please you to lie there, you may—but to no other place will I admit you."

"If we can do no better," returned the angel, "we must accept your ungracious offer."

They did so, and in the morning the angel, calling their host, said: "My friend, I give you this cup," and he presented to him the stolen goblet.

The hermit, more and more astonished at what he saw, said to himself, "Now I am certain this is the devil. The good man who received us with all kindness he despoiled, and gives the plunder to this fellow who refused us a lodging."

Turning to the angel, he exclaimed: "I will travel with you no longer. I commend you to God."

"Dear friend," answered the angel, "first hear me, and then go thy way. When thou wert in thy hermitage, the owner of the flock unjustly put to death his servant. True it is he died innocently, but he had formerly done deeds for which he deserved to die. God allowed him to be slain, to enable him to escape the future consequences of those former sins of which he had repented. But the guilty man who stole the sheep will suffer eternally, while the owner of the flock will repair, by alms and good works, that which he ignorantly committed. As for the son of the hospitable knight, whom I strangled in the cradle, know that before the boy was born he performed numerous works of charity and mercy, but afterwards grew parsimonious and covetous in order to enrich the child, of which he was inordinately fond. This was the cause of its death; and now its distressed parent again is become a devout Christian. Then, for the cup which I purloined from him who received us so kindly, know that before the cup was made, there was not a more abstemious person in the world; but afterwards he took such pleasure in it, and drank from it so often, that he was intoxicated twice or thrice during the day. I took away the cup, and he has turned to his former sobriety. Again, I cast the pilgrim into the river; and know that he whom I drowned was a good Christian but had he proceeded much farther, he would have fallen into a mortal sin. Now he is saved, and reigns in celestial glory. Then, that I bestowed the cup upon the inhospitable citizen, know nothing is done without reason. He suffered us to occupy the swine-house, and I gave him a valuable consideration. But he will hereafter reign in hell. Put a guard, therefore, on thy lips, and detract not from the Almighty. For He knoweth all things."

The hermit, hearing this, fell at the feet of the angel and entreated pardon. He returned to his hermitage, and became a good and pious Christian.

In the Middle Ages, woman was an object of condemnation by the church. She was the sink of iniquity, the source of all evil, the pestilence of men. A thirteenth-century anecdote shows that even Satan could not tolerate a woman, particularly a quarrelsome woman:

In human form, the demon was once in the service of a wealthy man. He performed his work so well that he was given his master's daughter as a wife. But the quarrels between husband and wife were so violent and so constant that after a year the demon begged permission to return to his own country. His master made tempting offers of wealth or anything else the demon might wish.

But without avail. The demon protested that he could not tolerate his quarrelsome wife any longer.

"I'd rather go back home," he said.

"Where's that?" his master asked.

"Hell," said the demon.

The Devil seemed fond of playing tricks on medieval clerics. Here is such a twelfth-century tale from the *Chronicle* of Florence of Worcester:

In the archbishopric of Trèves there was a fine monastery called Prumia, dedicated in honor of the holy apostles Peter and Paul. It was founded in ancient days by Pippin, king of the Franks, the father of Charlemagne. A strange event is said by all those who dwelt there to have happened as follows:

One morning the cellarer of this monastery with his servant entered the wine cellar in order, as was usual, to make a libation of wine at the altar. He found one of the casks, which the day before he had left full, up to the opening of the peg which is usually called the bung or the spigot, emptied and the wine pouring all over the flagstones. Deeply grieved at the loss of wine that had occurred, he sharply rebuked the servant who was standing by, saying he had been careless the previous evening in closing the peg tightly and hence the damage had occurred. With these words, he bade him under threat not to tell anyone what had happened. For he was afraid that, if the abbot should find out about this, he would contemptuously take this assignment away from him.

Late in the evening, before the brethren went to sleep, he went into the cellar and carefully tightened all the pegs in the wine casks. Then he closed the door and went to his couch.

In the morning when he went into the cellar as usual he observed that another cask was emptied as far as the hole in the peg, as on the previous day, and that the wine was pouring out. At sight of this, not knowing to whose negligence he should attribute the damage done, he bemoaned the incident deeply, completely amazed. Finally, he enjoined upon his servant not to tell anyone what had occurred. Before seeking his couch in the evening, he tightened all the pegs in the casks as carefully as possible, and sad and worried he went to bed. At dawn he rose, opened the cellar, and on the third day noticed that the spigot had been pulled out and that the wine had poured out through the hole. Hence, not without reason, he was terrified by what had happened and, afraid to keep silent any longer about the total loss of the wine, he hurried over to the abbot, threw himself at his feet, and informed him in sequence of what had occurred. The abbot held a council with the brethren and ordered the pegs in the casks containing the wine to be smeared all around, in the evening, with holy oil.

At daybreak the brother as usual went into the cellar and found there a remarkably tiny black boy clinging with his hands to one of the spigots. The cellarer quickly grasped him and brought him to the abbot.

"See, father," he cried, "this boy whom you see here created all the damage that we suffered in the storehouse."

Saying this, he described how he found the boy hanging on to a peg. The abbot, wondering at the incredible color and size of the little boy, held a council and gave orders for a monk's robe to be brought for him and to let him stay in the monastery with the schoolboys. This done, the boy, following the abbot's injunctions, accompanied the schoolboys night and day: but he never took food or drink, and spoke to nobody publicly or in private. At other times, in the quiet night and noonday hours, he would rest on his cot, weeping ceaselessly and sighing again and again.

Meanwhile an abbot of another monastery, coming to the same place to pray, remained there for a few days. When the schoolboys often passed by before him, as he was sitting with the abbot and the older monks of the monastery, the little boy, extending his hands to him, gazed at the abbot with tears as though he wanted to ask him something. As the boy repeated this performance several times, the abbot marveled at his diminutive size and asked those who were sitting beside him why they wanted to keep such a little boy in the monastery. Laughingly they answered: "This little boy is not what you think." And they related the damage he had inflicted and how he was found clutching with his hands at the spigot in the cask and how he had behaved among them.

On hearing this, the abbot became terrified and with a deep groan he said: "Drive him out of the monastery as quickly as possible or you may experience a greater loss or the utmost danger. For evidently he is the Devil hiding in human guise. But as you are protected by God's mercy through the merits of the saints whose relics are preserved here, he cannot harm you any further."

Straightway the boy was brought to the jurisdiction of the abbot of the monastery. When they took off his monk's robe, he vanished like smoke from between their hands.

The *Gesta Regum Anglorum*—the exploits of the kings of England—is a popular history of England by William of Malmesbury, who flourished in the twelfth century. One tale tells the story of a woman's wiles:

In these days something similar occurred, not as the result of a divine miracle but through demoniac stratagems. When I tell you the story, your belief will not waver, although listeners may be incredulous. I heard the tale from a man who swore he had been an eye-witness, and I would be ashamed to question him. There was a woman living in Berkeley, experienced, as was afterward evident, in witchcraft and knowledgeable in ancient auguries, a slave to her appetite, completely wanton, setting no limit to her misdeeds. She was still this side of advancing age, although she was closely entering and stepping on the threshold of decline.

One day, when she was dining, a crow that she kept as a pet uttered some cry or other more loudly than usual. On hearing this, the woman's knife fell from her hand and she grew pale. Uttering a groan, "This day," she said, "my plough has come to the last furrow. Today I have to bear and suffer a great loss."

As she said this, a messenger of evil came in and, when asked why he came in looking so glum, he said: "From the town I bring news of your son's death and his whole family. They perished in a sudden collapse of the house."

The woman was heartbroken at this lamentable news and fell down in a faint. Feeling sickness creeping through her body, she quickly wrote letters summoning her surviving children, together with a monk and a nun. Sobbing, she addressed them when they came: "My sons, on account of my pitiful fate I have always been attached to demoniac arts. I was the dregs of all the vices, the mistress of every enticement. However, in the midst of these crimes, there was hope of your devotion that soothed my poor soul. In my despair, I was depending on you and I imagined that you would be my defenders against the demons, my saviors against the most cruel enemies. Now, since I have reached the end of life and I shall have as the executors of my punishment those whom I had as advisors in my sin, I ask you, by the mother who nursed you, if you have any faith and any piety, at least to try to alleviate my torments. With regard to my soul you will not revoke the sentence that has been passed, but perhaps you will save my body in this manner. Sew me in a stag's skin, then set me on my back in a stone tomb: on top, place a stone of great weight all around, with three iron chains. Let fifty psalms be sung, and the same number of masses day and night, to check the fierce assault of the adversaries. Thus, if I rest without disturbance for three nights, on the fourth day dig your mother out of the ground; although I am afraid that the earth will refuse to receive and cherish me in its bosom, for it has so often resented my evil deeds."

Her orders were carried out, the sons putting all their energy into the task. But, alas! their devout tears were of no avail, nor their vows, nor their prayers: so great was the woman's evil, so great Satan's violence. For during the first two nights, when choirs of clerics chanted the psalms around the body, the demons without the slightest effort broke down one by one the door of the church which had been closed with a huge bolt, and tore away the two end chains. The middle one, which had been wrought more skilfully, remained unimpaired. On the third night around cockcrow the entire monastery seemed to be shaken from its foundations by the noise of the approaching enemy.

One of them, more horrifying than the others in appearance and taller in stature, shook the gates with greater force than the others and dashed it into fragments. The clerics grew rigid with fear, their hair stood on end, and their voices stuck in their throat. The taller fiend, with an arrogant gesture, as it appeared, approached the coffin, and calling out her name commanded her to arise. When she answered that she was unable to do so on account of the bonds, he said: "You will be freed, and to your own destruction."

Forthwith he broke the chain which had escaped the fury of the others, without any effort, as it was a hempen rope. With his foot he also pushed away the lid of the coffin. Then he grasped the woman by the hand and in sight of everyone dragged her out of the church. Then before the door a black spirited horse appeared and neighed. Iron hooks projected over its entire body. The wretched woman was placed on the hooks, and presently she vanished from the sight of everyone with the entire crew. But her cries could be heard for almost four miles, as she pitifully begged for help.

In medieval France there was a devout, retiring girl who was frightfully assaulted by Satan with lust of the flesh. Tearfully she prayed to be released from temptations. As she was once praying thus, an angel appeared to her in person and told her to repeat: "My flesh trembleth for fear of thee; and I am afraid of thy judgments." Then, he added: "You will be freed."

She recited the verse and presently temptation stopped. But, temptation returning, she prayed again.

"How is it with you?" asked the angel on his second appearance.

"Worse than before," she answered.

"You think you can live without temptation?" asked the angel. "You must choose one temptation that you prefer." "Since that is so, I select my first temptation. For although it was shameful, it was still a human temptation. The one I now experience is utterly demoniac."

"Repeat," commanded the angel, "this verse: "I have done judgment and justice: leave me not to mine oppressors."

She did so, and the Spirit of Blasphemy left her.

One of the remarkable features in the Middle Ages was the widespread presumption and actual belief that Judaism and Satanism were intimately connected.

In those times, Jews were penalized economically and politically, and socially they were ostracized, objects of contempt and hatred, in conformity with the traditional Christian attitude.

As the universal enemies of Christianity were Satan and the Jewish people who would not accept Christianity, the two adversaries of Christian doctrine merged together in the public mind as one consolidated opponent, so that the Jew became equated with Satan. The result was that in medieval legend and drama, in sculpture and paintings, the Jew was represented with fiendish features, with inherent diabolic traits, and with a Satanic nature. Such identifications appeared pictorially and visually throughout medieval Europe, but particularly in the Germanic regions. Satan, who is Antichrist, becomes Judaic. The goat, for example, is the alter image of the Satanic *persona*. The Jew therefore became pictorially a goat shape, endowed with hircine attributes.

In other directions, too, wherever there was evil, or crime, felony, murder, robbery, the Devil was the agent provocateur, the instigator, and ultimately the author himself. Hence all natural phenomena that were destructive—famine and plague and floods—were equally the work of the Evil Spirit. And, by a simple syllogistic conclusion, the Jews bore the brunt of these disasters. They were persecuted, condemned, punished as the image of Satan himself. It was, in a sense, a prolongation of the early Christian hatred, but it extended into the centuries, and even when the religious motif was not apparent, the Satan-Devil equation never lost its warped stability.

VI

THE DEVIL IN ART AND MUSIC

IN THE course of centuries there developed an urge among
people to look at the Devil, to see him eye to eye. For ages
he had been impalpable, though far more than a figment.
What was his visual reality? If that were discovered, men
would have a tangible enemy to grapple with, not a concept,
however sharply defined and confirmed. Among all peoples
came the compulsion to present him so that his identity
could never more be questioned. Was he a multi-shaped creature typifying the crimes and lusts and evil acts of men? Did
he present the same image everywhere? Was he an arrogantly
exultant anthropomorphic figure who towered above mankind, like some malefic Atlas? Was he like a triple-headed
Cerberus? Or a snaky mass that coiled around the earth? Or
one of the horrendous shapes that the poet Vergil describes
as cluttering up the gateway to Hades—Grief and Avenging
Cares and Wan Disease and Wretched Old Age and Fear and
Evil-Counseling Hunger and Foul Need, Shapes frightful to
see?

Satan was, in fact, all these forms, and more. His image,
however, changed with the generations. At times he even

assumed an almost heroic appearance, molded in human form. It was Christianity that shaped the Satanic concept into pictorial and sculptural reality. Through art, Satan attained his dimensional actuality. No longer could his existence be disputed. He was manifest. He was visual. He was the final image, the age-old thought, come to life.

In Christian art, Satan was first depicted in the sixth century. He is represented in frescoes and miniatures among the angelic hosts. He had not yet attained his more characteristic form and features. In the tenth century, in fact, Pope John XII, who was called the Boy Pope, was actually suspected of having a kindly feeling toward the fallen angel, for he was said to have offered Satan a libation.

Pictorially and visually, the Devil has been presented, since the Middle Ages, in a variety of imaginative, creative aspects. He stares from bas-reliefs. He is entwined in columnar church capitals. He is carved on choir benches. His infernal form recurs in many a church ornamentation. Predominantly, in the medieval church, he is a serpent with a human face. One medieval description of the Fiend, the basis of many woodcuts and other forms of illustration, runs as follows:

The Devil is like a bear or a lion tied to a stake. Although he walks about roaring, in his chains, he yet hurts no one, except a person whom he may catch within his reach. According to the Apostle Peter, he goes around as a roaring lion, seeking whom he may devour. He often terrifies and obstructs holy men, but he cannot harm them.

Satan, being multiform, is depicted in art with both anthropomorphic and theriomorphic characteristics, alternately human and animalistic. The goat, for instance, became a sculptural and pictorial image of Satan.

In Europe, particularly in the eastern regions, representations of the devil were often in bestial form, as a bull, or bear, or leopard.

In Western Europe, however, the Devil gradually assumed a more human or partly human form.

In early Christian art, Satan is depicted as a serpent. In the East the serpent is considered the very essence of evil. Robert Burns has a poem, *Address to the Deil,* in which the terror inspired by the Evil One is apparent.

By the thirteenth century, Satan is commonly depicted in sculpture, in miniatures and in other pictorial media as a serpent with a human head. Which means that there is something abnormally sinister in him, although he professes to display human traits. In the Baptistery in Florence and in the Campo Santo in Pisa the Devil so appears.

As a complete human form, he first appears on the ivory cover of the manuscript Gospels of Charles-le-Chauve. In an eleventh-century Greek manuscript, devils are equally human, but black in color.

On Mt. Athos, a cluster of Byzantine monasteries, ecclesiastical art paints Satan with a gigantic mouth, long protruding teeth. He is engaged in chewing up human beings, sinners who are in his toils. Standing in a red pool representing a flaming fire, he towers over his victims, who are writhing in the blood-red depths.

On the tower of Notre Dame in Paris Le Stryge is a diabolical sculptural figure, the Devil himself, the adversary, as he has always been, of orthodox religion, of all religion. On other sections of the towers there are hosts of such figures. It is a typical Devil, winged, with lolling tongue, horns, and a malevolent expression.

In one Italian church the Devil is a gross human form, with an ox head and eagle's claws. On his shoulders are mounted heads, belching flames.

On the walls of the Campo Santo there are swarms of fiendish shapes. In one instance, Satan is sitting in hell, in armor plate. Like Cerberus, he has three mouths, with which he crunches a victim. In his claws other sinners are grasped.

Beginning with the thirteenth century, Satan becomes, artistically, a milder figure—even, on occasion, a caricature. So he appears in Giotto and in the painters of Giotto's school. In one case, Satan is robed as a professor; again, as a monk, or a hermit, or a beautiful seductive female Devil.

Giles Fletcher, the sixteenth-century English poet, refers to this type of representation:

> A good old hermit he might seem to be,
> That for devotion had the world forsaken,
> And now was travailing some saint to see.

This differentiation of the Satanic form is illustrated again and again, in varying circumstances, in successive centuries. In the Bodleian Library, at Oxford University, a stained glass shows the Devil as a beautiful woman tempting St. Dunstan. On the walls of the Campo Santo, in Pisa, St. Paphnutius is similarly depicted.

In a fifteenth-century glass panel, at Riom, the Devil is represented as a woman tempting St. Mars.

Martin Schoengauer (c. 1423–1491) has a copper-plate engraving of St. Anthony assaulted by Satan and his devils.

Satan accusing Job is a fresco by Daniele de Volterra appearing in the Campo Santo in Pisa.

Gustave Doré produced an impressive Satan meditating and philosophizing in Miltonic strain. "High on a throne . . . Satan exalted sat."

Franz Simm, who illustrated Goethe's Faust, has Faust signing the Satanic contract with blood. Faust, in academic robes, is drawing blood from his left arm, while Satan looks on interestedly.

Hell is sculptured on the main entrance at Bourges, in France. In the same place, also of the fourteenth century, is a sculptured Last Judgment, with a profusion of diabolic figures.

A German artist executed a Christ in Hell, surrounded by demons.

Albrecht Dürer made a woodcut of the Woman of Abomination according to the *Revelation* of St. John the Divine.

In all these artistic productions, the Devil and his demons are always present.

The nineteenth-century German artist Schnorr von Carolsfeld has a Jesus casting out Devils.

Heaven and Hell often appear in medieval Bible illustrations and in German woodcuts, with Satan again in dramatic prominence.

Salvator Rosa has St. Anthony fighting the Devil. Gustave Doré executed Dante's Ice Hell, with the brooding batwinged demon in the foreground.

There are many paintings, etchings, woodcuts of the witches' Sabbat, with men and women dancing, cavorting, and disporting themselves or riding through the air by moonlight, while the Goat-Demon presides on his throne.

A twelfth-century *Hortus Deliciarum,* written for the edification of monks, contains numerous pictorial scenes. One illustration depicts Satanic temptations that lure away ascetics from the *corona vitae*—the crown of life. Among such temptations are included lavish dress, city life, worldly comforts, laziness, money.

Again, he is a dragon or a griffin, with lolling tongue and prehensile claws and a fearsome expanse of sable wings. He is a monstrous form attended by unclean and loathsome familiars, by sinister cats and furtive creatures from the fantastic bestiary of medieval horrors. Skulls and charnel-house murkiness surround him. His heraldic insignia are Death and Disaster. A fourteenth-century Florentine painter has a fresco of Satan, depicted with three faces, a symbolic perversion of the Trinity. Satan is thus represented, three-faced, in miniatures, in manuscript illuminations, and in sculpture. It was a popular medieval image of the Fiend; for Dante, too, in the *Inferno*, Canto 34, declares:

> I did spy upon his head three faces.

With Vergil as his guide in Hell, Dante sees this triple-headed Lucifer chewing, with his three mouths, Cassius and Brutus, the assassins of Julius Caesar, and Judas the Betrayer.

He is a winged satyr, piping his shrill, seductive notes on his magic horn. He is a half-human repulsive creature, furnished with swine's tusks, shaggy-haired, grasping a rakelike object, guarding hoards of treasure. He appears at the bed of dying sinners, attempting, with his cajoling forked tongue, to lure away souls into his own keeping. He is represented as a prisoner, confined in bonds, writhing like a fiendish Laocoon, while dwarfish satellites swarm around him. At times the Fiend is pictured as deformed in shape, ugly and revolting in appearance; for ugliness was equated with evil. Sometimes, again, he becomes a towering black creature.

In another illustration, his Satanic Majesty sits enthroned in a penumbrous gloom, encircled by shrieking hags, young and handsome initiates into sorcery. The locale is a forest grove, an arena for unholy contorted raptures. Ghoulish feasts and bloody libations glorify his demoniac person. On the ground lie in disarray smashed skulls, gangrenous, half-bitten limbs, fragments of sacrificial infants.

In an ebony-pillared chamber the Supreme Demoniac Sovereign, winged and with hands outstretched, stands addressing his legions of spirits and elementals, the furtive denizens of hellish haunts. Shadowy too, and equipped with Stygian wings, they stand attentive like martial troops. This nightmarish macabre conception is Gustave Doré's contribution to the Satanic saga. Medieval woodcuts and etchings depict the horned monstrosity being offered allegiance, as karcists and witches, necromancers and other adepts in the occult approach him to swear allegiance. In one woodcut the Archfiend is shown urging his dedicated adherents to trample on the cross in a pagan rite.

Apart from woodcut illustrations in antique demonographic treatises, artists through the centuries have been attracted imaginatively by the Satanic scene and its visual implications and possibilities.

In Italy, Giotto (c. 1266–1337), noted for his remarkable series of religious frescoes, produced *The Last Judgment.* It depicts Christ as the central figure, while in the foreground grovel the damned souls. A horrifying Satan, crunching the wicked, represents the arch adversary, evil and powerful. In the same century the goldsmith and artist Orcagna executed a similar scene in Santa Maria, in Florence.

From one age to another, from century to century, this compulsive appeal of the demoniac motif offered itself to sculptor and painter and architect. And the roster extends, endless. Nor are the imaginative renderings repeated. They become individualized, wrought into uniqueness by the artist's personal conception of his subject. The tradition continues, from Giotto to Dürer, from Hieronymus Bosch to Gustave Doré. And in the Orient as well, both the Chinese and the Japanese execute the demoniac motif. An eighteenth-century Chinese illustration, for instance, depicts magicians practicing their skill, while a toad-familiar looks on. Kasuo Kuniyoshi, the Japanese artist, has the Witch Omibaba perform an operation on a victim. Skulls are strewn around, and in the background looms a flaming apparition. It is the old medieval conception, but with an Oriental touch, a Nipponese sensitivity. And in each case the infernal agents, the dread confrontations and the figures and accessories of the occult are readily recognizable despite certain national or ethnic peculiarities.

In the medieval line stands Stefano de Giovanni Sassetta (c. 1392–1450), one of the greatest Sienese painters of his century. His subjects were mainly religious, but even then, or possibly because of this trend, he touched closely on the Satanic cycle. In his *St. Anthony Tormented by Demons*, a painting in tempera on wood, the saint, lying supine but still defiant, is assailed and lashed by weird birdlike forms. Funereal trees surround the monastery. Dark shaggy things advance upon the holy man with writhing snakes in their hands.

Another Italian, Benozzo Gozzoli (1420–1498), a Florentine painter, was noted for his inventiveness in detail and the wide range of his subjects: courtiers and animals, landscapes and pageantry. He also executed an impressive *St. Peter and Simon Magus*. Simon Magus is the sorcerer who appears in the *Acts of the Apostles* 8. He bewitched the people of Samaria and practiced levitation. Gozzoli represents him hovering high in a vaulted chamber, to the amazement of the bystanders. Simon received his power from the forces of evil and was thus able to oppose the laws of nature.

Another Florentine painter, Sandro Botticelli (c. 1445–1510), illustrated with eighty-four drawings, including infernal scenes and figures, Dante's *Divine Comedy*.

In Germany, Albrecht Dürer (1471–1528) was the leading artist in the German Renaissance. In addition to many notable works with religious motifs, he executed paintings on Satanic operations. One such picture is the *Knight, Death, and the Devil*, a common theme in medieval legend and ballad. He has also an engraving on *Death and the Devil*. *The Four Witches* extends his concern in occult matters, while his *Key of the Bottomless Pit* is wilder in tone and more haunting.

Italian art was prolific in the subject, and a prominent representative was Luca Signorelli (1441–1523). He was the leading painter of the Umbrian Renaissance school. Apart from his monumental religious frescoes and mythological subjects, as well as his striking nudes, he executed a *Souls of the Damned.* It presents a swarming mass of forms in contortions, symbolic of the agonies and tortures of life itself, and embracing skeletal shapes and demoniac figures. Michelangelo's *The Last Judgment* similarly swarms with demons. In a number of Italian paintings it is the multitude of Satan's satellites that produces the effect of the boundless power of their Master, and sometimes the absence of the Archfiend himself stresses his sinister and ubiquitous immanence.

The most outstanding artist of the early Dutch Renaissance was Hieronymus Bosch (c. 1462–1515). His special field was religious and allegorical subjects. He executed also strange representations of demons and other monsters, grim and gruesome figures of horrendous import.

Devils again appear in Luca Signorelli's work at Orvieto, human in shape. The Cathedral of Chartres, on the other hand, has sculptured diabolical figures with horns, claws, and tail.

In the palace of the Doges, in Venice, Paul Veronese has a lavish Satanic fresco, the largest in existence.

In crucifixion paintings, black devils often appear, and bearded satyrs, and bat-winged creatures, a mixture of classical mythological features together with early Christian conceptions of demons. Niccolo di Pietro so represented the fiends. In the following century, the fifteenth, Gaudenzio Ferrari shows their mere ugliness at Vercelli. In another crucifixion, by Tommaso Masaccio, the Florentine painter, the artist endows the fiend with bat wings.

In illuminated manuscripts, notably in the *Ars Moriendi* —The Art of Dying—devils disport themselves evilly. On a Saxon stone, in northern England, three devils are seen clutching the soul of a dying man.

Hans Baldung (c. 1475–1545), important in the German Renaissance, produced a striking Sabbat scene, with the congregation of witches and familiars awaiting the Master in an encircling tenebrous atmosphere.

Another artist who displayed interest in the arcana of the Black Arts was the Flemish painter Quinten Matsijs (c. 1466–1530). In his study of an alchemist he reproduces all the infernal apparatus and aids, with grimoires and skulls complete.

Michael Herr, a German artist who also flourished in the sixteenth century, paints a Sabbat that takes place in the Blacksberg, in Germany, which was actually the locale of many witch assemblies. All the usual trappings and trimmings are in evidence, testimony of the widespread traditions of the Master's activities.

In the seventeenth century Peter Brueghel the Younger appears (1564–1638). He was known as Höllenbrueghel— The Infernal Brueghel—because many of his paintings depicted infernal scenes. In the *Witch of Malleghem,* for example, a witch is, strangely enough, performing the beneficent act of healing the sick. Her paraphernalia lie around: particularly phials and strange concoctions that owe their efficacy to her alliance with the occult powers.

A contemporary was Rijckaert David (1612–1662), a Flemish artist. He depicts an alchemist who is so versed in occult practices that he has just created an android with demoniac aid. In another painting, the Sabbat, there is a gathering of witches, along with their attendant familiars in the form of lizards, cats, and toads. The assembly is paying reverence to Satan, while in the near foreground St. James the Elder is opposing sinister powers.

Salvatore Rosa (1615–1673) follows the same trend. He is noted particularly for his landscapes and battle scenes, but he showed a profound interest in the Occult as well. In his *The Witch of Endor,* a brooding execution, the witch is exorcising the spirit of King David.

David Teniers (1610–1690), the Dutch artist, has a pastoral scene in which the artist's wife has her fortune told by chiromancy. Another work of his shows an alchemist absorbedly consulting an occult treatise. Again, in an alchemical laboratory, the alchemist himself is perusing a grimoire, a manual of magic. In the *Departure for the Sabbat,* Teniers reproduces the elaborate preparations for the approaching infernal congregation.

Jean Antoine Watteau (1684–1721), the French painter noted for his pastoral scenes, country dances, and rustic life, also produced, in the Three Witches, a lurid study of diabolic abandonment.

Another Frenchman, Jean Fragonard (1732–1806), known for his romantic canvases, has an unusual sketch of Satan in a state of terror at the sight of a woman exposing her body. This is a case of the Evil One himself having his own practices turn against himself.

Ascetic restraint confronted by feminine seductiveness appears in The Temptation of St. Anthony, by Domenico Morelli (1826–1901), the historical and genre painter.

Of all those artists who brought artistic reality to the Satanic concept and demonstrated the impact of the Fiend upon human affairs, the most amazing personality, touched with a wild genius, was Francisco Goya (1746–1828), the Spanish painter. He is famous both for the tumultuous vicissitudes of his own life and his depiction of the national court life of his time. But he is equally noteworthy for his almost mystical concentration on occult themes, demoniac phenomena, and the satirical presentation of the wild ways of fiends and warlocks, necromancers and ghouls. He depicts witches and demons in a vast variety of aspects and poses and confrontations. He creates, in fact, an occult, diabolic world, where the most ghastly abnormalities are a common practice. This world is marked by weird concepts and equally fantastic purposes that materialize into dread beings, bat-winged demons, corpses rising from moldering graves, flights of aged and youthful sorceresses galloping through the nocturnal clouds, congregations of devotees of the Sabbat rites, goat-shaped fauna accepting human fealty. It is an awesome, furtive universe that Goya makes visible and manifest. He creates ghostly, bestial faces, creatures half-human, half-animal, skeletal vestiges that belong to the dark spirits of the night, to a monstrous Nether Region, to an unearthly zone haunted by Satan and his numberless minions.

The Gathering of the Sorcerers is characteristically Goya. Against a crescent moon and darkling clouds, goat-faced, goat-horned, and crowned, Satan, hircine and evil, sits enthroned among his votaries, the witches who are paying homage to their Master. A bony figure of a child sprawls on the ground, while one witch presents a child as a human sacrifice to the Fiend.

In another painting three bestial elemental spirits are grouped together, denizens of the occult domain. Again, elsewhere, a witch, attended by cats who are her familiars, is sacrificing a human being to the goat-fiend. On the ground near her a vessel stands ready to receive the victim's blood.

When we enter the nineteenth century, we note certain changes in the Satanic concept. Pictorially, it is less crude, less dependent on the medieval accessories of shadowy hosts, contorted fiends, Sabbats and the material paraphernalia that had long been associated with demoniac representations. Now we find a more poetic design, stripped of skulls and grimoires. The Satanic idea acquires a more mystical, a more symbolic character. William Blake (1757–1827), the English poet and mystic, illustrates this kind of trend. He depicts symbolically the conflict between Man and Evil, a conflict that goes back to the dualism, as we saw before, represented by Ahura Mazda, the beneficent deity, and Ahriman, the Satanic Spirit of Evil.

Still later than Blake, Gustave Doré (1833–1893), the

French artist, was haunted by the Miltonic Lucifer. The Demon lies prone, jet wings outspread, in a meditative pose. Around him are, in a kind of amphitheatrical form, clustering boulders and stalactites, with puny human figures leaning or standing or crouching among the rocks. In the *Sovereign of the Infernal Hosts* the Master Fiend is shown among his legions, in ranks crowding up to his very presence. Again, the Archfiend is represented as a winged creature, flying over the whirling universe, dominant and baleful and potent as ever.

Perhaps it was during the Renaissance that art was most profoundly conscious of the Fiend as an entity and of his malignant presence among men. In the lavishness and luxury and licentiousness of Italian culture and, on the other hand, in the ascetic and monastic simplicities of the devout and the religiously dedicated, Satan found rich and ready scope for his intrusions, his temptations, his wiles. And he always appears rampant or elusive or enwrapped in his darksome aura, more than man, less than a god.

But in China, in more recent times, he assumes the role of craftsman, in the field of the applied arts. And his specialty is ceramics. There is a type of fretwork carving on porcelain that was long known as *kuei kung*—Devil's work. The name arose from the fact that the delicate carving demonstrated the exceptional and almost more than human skill of the potter. And, with Oriental politeness and a sense of humility, the Chinese were eager to give the Devil his due.

The old folk legends of Scotland and Brittany, of Ireland, Italy, and Germany, as well as the tales told in remote Asiatic regions, are full of the Devil's appeal. For in his musical role he can be amazingly appealing. His enticing notes can lure to destruction, and his eerie melodies that creep and weave furtively through the nocturnal landscape, when everything impossible may happen, are fraught with unnamed terrors for human beings. Yet Satan can be a jolly fiddler as well, or produce jigs and capers with his bagpipes.

And he is, in either capacity, as compulsive as the Pied Piper himself.

In this respect, then, Satan realizes his power and is quite well aware of his ready ability to play on the will and the emotions of his prospective victims.

Satan has an appreciation of the influence of music on the human spirit. And he often lends himself to wild and whirling and seductive harmonies, to tumultuous sarabands that enliven themselves in the notes of a piano or the twanging strings of a violin. Satan is the fiddler who can make you dance to his tune. He is an expert virtuoso. He can also play the bagpipes, extracting weird and bewildering melodies that haunt the listener and lead him to his doom. He can send you into dangerous dream states with his banjo. Music, in short, is only another of Satan's methods of possessing men.

In Central Europe, in the Balkans and the Carpathian Mountains, along the banks of the Danube and on the Hungarian steppes, there were many legends in which a peasant fiddler or a gypsy flute player was said to have acquired his strangely alluring harmonies from the Fiend himself. The Devil is in the strings, the rumor went around. It is the Devil's music, the whispers went. Or the Fiend has taught him these abandoned rhythms.

One of the most tumultuous compositions is Giuseppe Tartini's Il Trilli del Diavolo—The Devil's Sonata. Tartini (1692–1770) was a remarkable violinist. His early life was wildly irregular, and in turn he was attracted to the church, to law, to the profession of arms. Later, inspired by a dream in which he heard the Devil play with exquisite impeccability, he composed his *Devil's Sonata*. He himself gives an account of that dream:

One night in 1713 I dreamt that I had made a compact with the devil, who promised to be at my service on all occasions.

At last I thought I would offer my violin to the devil. To my great astonishment I heard him play a solo so singularly beautiful . . . that it surpassed all the music I had ever heard or conceived in the whole course of my life. . . . The violence of the sensation awoke me; instantly I seized my violin in the hopes of remembering some portion of what I had heard, but in vain! The work which this dream suggested . . . is doubtless the best of all my compositions.

Satan has even intruded into musical terminology. The expression *diabolus in musica*—the devil in music—concedes Satan's interest in the musical sphere. The phrase is a nickname for the tritone. The tritone is the interval of three whole notes considered in musical theory as the "most dangerous" interval.

Apart from Tartini's experience, too, the Devil is a musical connoisseur. In operas, symphonies, and occasional compositions, the Evil One can introduce his satellites into a demoniac scene. Or he himself plays a primary role. In Mozart's *Don Giovanni,* for instance, demons appear, as in *Faust,* and drag Giovanni down to Hell.

The Satanic musical cooperation continues. In 1731 Charles Coffrey produced in London a ballad opera under the name of *The Devil to Pay, or the Wives Metamorphos'd.*

Le Village du Devin—The Village Soothsayer—was an opera composed by Jean Baptiste Rousseau, a French poet, who produced it in 1752.

The nineteenth century is markedly a Satanic century. It was manifest in 1830, when Hector Berlioz produced his *Symphonie Fantastique,* the last movements of which depict a witches' Sabbat. George Macfarren's *The Devil's Opera* was produced in London in 1836. The composition is a satire on the diabolical elements in works such as Weber's *Freischütz,* Meyerbeer's *Robert le Diable,* and Robert Heinrich Marschner's opera entitled *The Vampyr.*

Paganini, like Tartini before him, experienced romantic adventures that created a Mephistophelian aura about his name. He gained a reputation for the weird melodic variations of his works. They were, it was said, the result of an alliance with his Satanic ally. *Le Streghe,* in particular— *The Witches' Dance*—for violin and orchestra, offers such an occult interpretation. Once, in fact, after Paganini had played in Vienna, some members in the audience declared that the Fiend had actually been seen guiding the violinist's fingers. Talk about this alleged incident grew so insistent that in 1828 Paganini was forced to publish a letter written by his mother in confirmation of his human origin.

Similarly, Jacques Offenbach, the German composer who became a French citizen, was stimulated to Satanic themes. His operetta *Orphée aux Enfers* belongs in this category. Franz Liszt too produced a Mephisto Waltz, diabolic and unique, shattering in its impact. In Wagner also, the diabolic motif is manifest. In his Tannhäuser the shining minnesinger himself falls in love with the goddess Venus turned demon.

The Devil's name and his evident influence appear in quite a number of musical works. An opera by Anton Dvorak, for instance, is called *The Devil and Kate.* Eduard Nápravník, the Czech-born naturalized Russian composer who died in 1915, executed a symphony based on Lermontov's *The Demons.* In 1938 Arthur Benjamin produced in London an opera entitled *The Devil Take Her.* Still later, in 1950, at his death, Vincenzo Tommasin left a ballet under the name of *Le Diable S'amuse,* based on themes by Paganini.

VII

SATANIC POSSESSION, EXORCISM, VISIONS, TEMPTATIONS

In the history of Christian thought in particular, but also in the history of other faiths, demoniac possession meant that a human being was under some allegedly supernatural control. The symptoms of such a condition were shrieks and groans on the victim's part, twisting of the body into inconceivable contortions, horrible grimaces, cataleptic fits, howlings like those of animals, blasphemies, prophetic pronouncements, the utterance of words in a strange tongue not previously known to the possessed. In addition, the demoniac displayed an abnormal appetite that craved nauseating and excrementitious food, and a physical strength far beyond the victim's usual capacity.

The condition itself was not unfamiliar in antiquity, in Greece and other parts of Europe. In Greece, for example, the Pythian priestess of Apollo at the temple of Delphi was possessed, filled with the inspiration of the god. In that state she made oracular forecasts.

Exorcism is an adjuration, addressed to the Evil Spirit, to

abandon the body of the person so possessed. Erasmus, the great medieval humanist, wrote a piece on Exorcisms, but he did so with his tongue in his cheek. On the other hand, there is extant a Latin treatise that describes various types of exorcism and gives assurance of their efficacy.

Sometimes exorcism was successful, and thousands of obscene devilish creatures would stream out from the bodies of afflicted persons. It might chance, however, that exorcism was abortive. This happened in the case of St. Eustachia, who was possessed by devils all her life.

Christ exorcised evil spirits, and the Christian church regularly used a ceremonial ritual to expel demons. There is a case of possession in *Luke* 8:26–30:

When he saw Jesus, he cried out, and fell down before him, and with a loud voice said, What have I to do with thee, Jesus, thou Son of God most high: I beseech thee, torment me not. For he had commanded the unclean spirit to come out of the man, for oftentimes it had caught him: and he was kept bound in fetters; and he brake the chains, and was driven of the devil into the wilderness.

And Jesus asked him, saying, What is thy name? And he said, Legion: because many devils were entered into him.

Another case of possession occurs in *Matthew* 8:28–32:

And when he was come to the other side into the country of the Gergesenes, there met him two possessed with devils, coming out of the tombs, exceeding fierce, so that no man might pass by that way. . . And he said unto them, Go. And when they were come out; they went into the herd of swine.

In the early centuries of Christianity the power of exorcism was considered a personal talent, and exorcism might be performed by anyone known to have the virtue of driving out an evil spirit from the corporeal frame of some hapless victim. But from the third century on, professional exorcists came into vogue. They were officially and formally entrusted with this function by the ecclesiastical authorities.

The elaborate rite of exorcism in Roman Catholicism is contained in the *Rituale Romanum*. St. Anthony was tempted by the devil on several occasions, but without success. Disappointed, Satan changed into a little black boy—a crafty device that was frequently employed by the Fiend. Again, the Devil appeared as a monk, coaxing the saint to take bread during a fast. Sometimes the Evil One took the form of a wild beast, terrifying by his ferocity, or of a swaggering soldier, or an enticing woman. The recluse in the desert, or in his cell, would behold a voluptuous girl. He would be assailed by lascivious gestures, lewd contortions, intolerable fleshly delights. Or Satan would offer gold and silver, worldly goods, luscious food. Or he would oppress an anchorite with spectral shapes, phantasmal images. This was Satan's method of retaliation, challenging the beneficence of the Divinity, subduing inherent goodness. But in the case of St. Anthony, and many another saint, he was never successful in possessing either the body or the spirit of the man of God. St. Bridget of Sweden and St. Hilarion, St. Benedict and St. Thomas Aquinas were likewise exposed to the artifices of Satan. In the agony of the infernal impacts, the medieval *Lives of the Saints* relate, many holy men, overcome by sinful desire, castrated themselves while others attempted suicide, not seldom successfully.

Gregory the Great, when consecrating an Arian church for Roman Catholic worship, exorcised the Devil with sacred relics. With a great clattering noise, Satan immediately vanished in the form of a huge pig.

There were other means of keeping Satan at bay. Charms were used, or the perfume of a black dog's gall. There is an allusion to a rustic charm in Robert Herrick's *Hesperides:*

> In the morning when ye rise,
> Wash your hands and cleanse your eyes;
> Next, be sure the water farre,
> For as farre as that doth light,
> So farre keeps the evil spright.

Certain plants had apotropaic virtues intended to frustrate the Devil or to counteract his influence. Henbane, vervain, modirworth, pimpernelle, betony, baldmony, laurel were often efficacious. Church bells were reputed to dispel evil spirits. Pilgrims of the Eastern Church, visiting Jerusalem, carried their shrouds with them. The shrouds acted as a protection against the Fiend.

A dish of salt used to be placed, in England, on the body of a deceased person: Salt was the symbol of immortality and eternity.

Moslems threw stones at the Devil. The first two words of St. John's Gospel, *In principio*, written on a paper and worn around the neck, acted as a charm against Satan.

In the early days of the Irish Church a saint's hymn was recited. It was known as Luirech, a holy protection. The Deer's Cry, the Hymn of St. Patrick, was most frequently used for this purpose.

In the twelfth century the Gospels too were repeated after Mass, with the same intent. "It helps to drive away ghosts," declares Giraldus Cambrensis, the Welsh geographer and historian, in his *Gemma Ecclesiastica*.

In Scotland, farmers used to leave part of their fields un-tilled. This land was known as *the good man's croft*. It was dedicated to Satan who, possessing it, would be indulgent to the other fields in their productivity.

In the fourth century the formula for exorcism was The Holy Name and the sign of the cross. Origen, the Christian writer and Father of the Greek Church, says that the fiends are afraid when they observe Christians wearing the cross.

Later, in the fifteenth century, papal directions for divert-
ing devils required the use of holy water, salt, and lighted
tapers.

The *Lives of the Saints* are full of accounts of Satanic
impacts. Anchorites in the deserts of Egypt or Syria, monks
at prayer in their cells, brethren laboring in the fields, in the
refectory, in the kitchen, walking along a country lane,
scribes copying ancient manuscripts, nuns in the midst of devotions—all felt the putrescent, corrupting aura of Satan's
manifestations. Sometimes a temptation, trifling in appearance and insignificant in itself, led to monstrous pride, to
wilfulness, to carnal lusts, and ultimately to total ruination.
Satan had innumerable ways, subtle and alluring by the
presumptive and apparent absence of sinister aftermaths, of
soul-searing intent. A medieval tale points up the possibility
of resisting him, compelling him actually to retract his temptation:

There was a girl of Nivelles in Brabant who, because of her
love of Christ, left the home of her parents. She joined the nuns
of the province and lived with them by the work of her hands,
dedicating herself to prayer and fasting.

The Devil, being jealous of her virtuous character, took a
goose from her father's place and set it down on the bench where
she was sitting with the other nuns. "Why do you torture
yourself with hunger, you poor girl?" he said. "Take this goose
and eat it."

She replied: "I am not permitted to eat it, because it was
stolen."

To which the Devil retorted: "Not at all. I took it from your
father's house."

The girl said: "You cannot deny that it was theft. Take the
goose quickly and give it back where you took it."

Seeing that it was of no avail, the Devil lifted up the goose, in
the presence of the nuns, and returned it to the house from
which he had taken it.

Her father's entire household testified that they heard a great din among the geese both when the Devil took the goose and when he returned it.

Even Christ himself had an encounter with Satan, when the Devil tempted him:

> Again, the devil taketh him up into
> an exceeding high mountain, and
> sheweth him all the kingdoms of the
> world, and the glory of them:
>
> And saith unto him, All these
> things will I give thee, if thou
> wilt fall down and worship me.
> MATTHEW 4:8–9

Satan went even further. In the presumed image of Christ, he presented himself once before Brother Rufinus, a fourth-century theologian. When the Fiend opened his mouth, Rufinus threw excrement into it. Immediately, Satan vanished, disappearing into a rock.

In the form, too, of Asmodeus, the demon of lust, Satan tries to work his evil way. Asmodeus, in his original Persian name, was Aeshma Daeva, the Spirit of Evil. In *Tobit* 3:7–8, Asmodeus attempts to prevent Sara's marriage because he himself is in love with her. In his jealousy, he murders her seven bridegrooms, one after the other, on Sara's wedding night:

> Sara the daughter of Raguel was also reproached by her father's maids: Because that she had been married to seven husbands, whom Asmodeus the evil spirit had killed, before they had lain with her. Dost thou not know, said they, that thou hast strangled thine husbands? Thou hast had already seven husbands, neither wast thou named after any of them.

It is difficult for man to circumvent Satan at all times. For he is, as a Christian poet of the fourth century declared, a juggler. He juggles with events, with promises, with scenes and earthly objects, with bodies and souls and circumstances. He gives everything a meretricious semblance of truth and virtue, and then he falsifies all that he says and does. But then it is usually too late. The evil has been done. One must therefore be continuously on the alert, and even the holy men and women were caught unaware.

But they punished and benumbed their lustful, rebellious flesh. For was it not the mere carapace of the eternal soul? By vigil and flagellation, by oraisons and toil, by abstention from bodily nourishment they subjugated their obsessive and evilly inspired longings. Thus, gasping and exhausted, they emerged triumphant from the diabolic infestations, unsullied and virtuous. And, in his frustration and disappointment, Satan danced an agonized jig.

Satan has, however, mastery over countless plans and maneuvers. He is mischievous. He plays childish pranks. He steals. He extinguishes candles during prayer. Or a lamp in a monk's cell. He makes off with poultry. Or cattle mysteriously disappear from a farmer's homestead. Masquerading in human image, or as a beast of the fields, the Devil lurks everywhere, tempting the weak and the innocent and the adventurous. He empties a granary in a monastery. And how numerous are the lamentations in old monkish chronicles of the Evil One spoiling food and drink. Satan assails with his amorphous hordes of demons of the night. Hoarse-voiced, they shriek and gibber and snap, responsive to the Archfiend's direction. He himself kidnaps a devout woman in the midst of her oraisons, setting her down on some distant waste land, bewildered, bereft of reason. Or he thrusts an aged anchorite into a deep well. Or dashes him to the ground, with excruciating fiendishness, from some towering mountain height. For Satan's pranks are never quite innocuous, and they never coincide with human playfulness. There is, in fact, no limit to his untiring ingenuity, no method of persecution or torture that is beyond his inventiveness.

Brueghel the Elder, the sixteenth-century Flemish painter, shows in his Sabbat picture St. James the Elder resisting Satanic attacks. St. Theresa of Spain, like many of the early mystics, saw visions of hell and the malevolent Satanic power and his baleful minions. But she too remained untouched, unbending, confronting and subduing the Devil with her own righteous will.

The story of the Dybbuk has attracted universal interest. The term *Dybbuk* itself signifies an attachment. In Jewish folklore it is the wandering soul that enters a living body and remains there until exorcised.

The superstition of the Dybbuk, made popular through the mystical Kabala and the corpus of Judaic lore, spread throughout Eastern Europe. There is, however, Biblical mention of this phenomenon. King Saul's melancholia is considered to have been due to the entrance of an evil spirit, driven out ultimately by David's music.

The Essenes were an ancient Jewish sect, composed of men who were recluses living in settlements similar to monasteries. They spent their days in religious study and mysticism and were reputed to be knowledgeable in exorcising those who were possessed. In the *Apocrypha* 6:1617, Raphael instructs Tobit in the procedure required in exorcism:

And when thou shalt come into the marriage chamber, thou shalt take the ashes of perfume, and shalt lay upon them some of the heart and liver of the fish, and shalt make a smoke of it.

And the devil shall smell it, and flee away, and never come again any more. . . .

The Jewish historian Josephus relates that a certain Eleazar could free a demon-ridden man. A contemporary of Josephus, the famous Johanan ben Zakkai, alludes to the method of exorcism:

We bring roots and make them smoke under the possessed: then we sprinkle water upon him, and the demon flees.

With this ritual may be compared the ritual described above in Tobit.

The kabalistic book entitled the *Zohar* comments on the practice:

If the soul, assuming a human shape on earth, does not acquire the experience for which it has made its heavenly descent and becomes contaminated, it must re-inhabit a body again until it can ascend, purified by repeated experiences.

In the sixteenth century, belief in the Dybbuk became an established credo. In the legend of *The Dybbuk,* the demoniac spirit that entered the body of a Jewish woman was exorcised before the devout and learned men of the synagogue, according to ancient, traditional ceremonies involving kabalistic mysticism, the utterance of the most sacred name of the Divinity, the Shemhamphoras, the seventy-two divine names. The thaumaturgic Rabbi then strove to extract the evil spirit by prayer and supplication. A dramatic presentation of the theme appears in A. Anski's *The Dybbuk,* which has been translated into several languages and performed effectively in many countries.

In some cases it was possible for Satan to be driven out by the resistant spirit of the person assailed. In India and Ceylon, Devil Dances are performed for the express purpose of exorcising evil spirits in the case of sick persons.

One of the major activities of Satan was to enter a human body and mold the spirit within to his own ghastly and enigmatic will. A weak body would succumb and become virtually a Satanic satellite, as happened in the case of countless witches and warlocks. The Devil might enter even a dead person, a woman recently deceased, a criminal who had been hanged. He had no scruples, of course, no discriminations. Again, the victim might wrestle with all his power, and if his religious faith were deep and firm and his spirit potent enough, Satan might be humiliated and crushed and depart gnashing his teeth. This situation occurred frequently. In dreams and visions and vigils, saints experienced a confrontation with the insidious and destructive wiles of the Tempter. St. Martin, John of Damascus, St. Giles were so confronted. So were St. Romanus and St. Margaret, St. Everard, St. Eustachium, St. Colette. The Devil defiled them and thrashed them. He harassed them daily. He howled lewd songs at them. He dragged their bodies and tired their flesh, torturing them with hammers and fetters and gridirons.

One heretical sect that flourished in the fourth century, the Massalians or Rachites, believed that Satan had been successful and that he actually resided in their bodies.

Ricalmus, Abbot of Schonthal, wrote around 1270 a book in Latin describing the deceits and stratagems practiced by demons on human beings in every minute circumstance, in every trivial movement, every thoughtless gesture. It is, asserts Ricalmus, the demon who is behind such annoyances and frustrations. It is he who lies in wait for absent-minded or indifferent or ignorant folk.

Variety is the Devil's motto. He is a hideous black lamb. He may appear as a handsome youth. Or a stone. Or a tree. He may tempt the appetite with a bunch of grapes or a brimming goblet of wine. And of course the object of such assaults is usually a devout monk or a nun, because, if Satan is successful, he is at the same time indirectly successful in his conflict with the Supreme Divinity.

In the thirteenth century, Caesar of Heisterbach, a Cistercian monk, produced a collection of miraculous tales that were immensely popular in the Middle Ages. The following story illustrates the holy man's need of humility: Once a church was desecrated by the presence of the Devil. The Prior approached him, along with a chaste young man who was very opinionated. The Prior addressed the Demon: If this young man orders you to leave the body, how will you dare to remain?

The Demon replied: I am not afraid of him, for he is filled with pride.

And Heisterbach, as usual, draws the moral that chastity without humility is of little avail before God or Devil. Satan gloats over clerics who succumb, even in their religious duties, to pride. And he consequently appears to them in apparitions, disdainfully, exultantly.

Once, some brethren who were singing in church loudly but without devotion, and raising their clamorous voices, were observed by a cleric. He happened to be nearby, and when he saw a demon standing on a higher spot and holding a large, long sack in his left hand, he observed further that the demon with his right hand outstretched caught the voices of the singing brethren and put them in the sack. Their chanting over, they congratulated each other on having praised the Lord well and mightily. But the monk who had seen the manifestation said: You sing well, but a sack full. Surprised, they asked him what he meant. He explained the vision and adjured them to shun vainglory.

St. Theophilus the monk once fell under the power of the Demon, but he was saved by the Virgin Mary. Rutebeuf, a thirteenth-century French troubadour, described the incident in a miracle play entitled *Le Miracle de Théophile*. The Church of Souillac, in France, depicted the episode sculpturally.

How do demons enter human beings? Caesar of Heisterbach has a novitiate and a monk discuss the question:

NOVITIATE: Some men declare that demons are not within men but outside them, just as a fort is said to be besieged from the outside, not from within. Other authorities express the contrary opinion, following the word of the Savior, who said: Depart from him, foul spirit.

MONK: It is incorrect to say "depart," unless he is within. Both theories however are true: according to whether the demon can be in man and cannot be. For Satan cannot be in a human soul, as Gennadius declares in the chapter on church dogmas: We do not believe that the Demon, by his energy, that is, his operation, can corporeally enter the soul. It is possible for him alone who created it, to enter the soul.

NOVITIATE: Why then is the Devil said to enter a man's heart or to try to do so?

MONK: His only way of entering is by leading the mind into wickedness. Hence the expression: Entering through the evil angels. When the Devil is said to be in a person, we must understand this not with regard to the soul but the body, because in the hollow parts of the body and in the intestines where the refuse is contained the Devil can dwell.

NOVITIATE: I am now clear on this point. But tell me, are there still other ways whereby demons are wont to harm men?

MONK: Demons have a thousand methods of inflicting harm, four of which I shall reveal to you. They harm some people by making false promises. Others they harm through their satellites by undermining faith. They harm many by attacking them in the body, and still others—and this is more dangerous—by making them fall into sin.

There was, again, says the same chronicler, the demon who admitted having entered a woman's body because she had been given over to him by her husband:

Last year, when our Abbot was celebrating mass and the mass was just over, a woman possessed of the Devil was introduced. Over her head he recited the gospel on the ascension, and at the words: *They shall lay hands on the sick, and they shall recover,* when he had laid his hand on her head, the demon uttered such a terrible cry that we were all affrighted. Commanded to depart, the demon replied: The all Highest does not yet wish it so. When asked how he had entered, he did not reply, nor did he let the woman reply. Afterward she confessed that on her husband's saying in her disturbed mind, "Go to the Devil," she felt the Devil entering through her ear.

Again:

When a certain woman of Breisig was five years old, the Devil entered her in the following manner. One day, when she was taking milk, her father in a rage said: May you eat the Devil in your stomach. Presently the child felt his entrance and until she was an adult she was harassed by him. This year, through the services of the Apostles Peter and Paul, whose church she visited, she was freed.

It is strange that in these contemporary times there are fewer Satanic incidents in which the Devil specifically tempts and obsesses saintly characters. When one such incident occurs it is treated as a rare novelty. It may be that saintly characters have established an indurated resistance to diabolic assaults. It may be that in these instances the Devil is really defeated or at least diverted, realizing his abortiveness.

Furthermore, in our present social and economic frame, the human objectives are clearly defined, and man need not waver or be misled, by whatever furtive operation, from these goals. And these goals are definitely commercial, industrial, social, financial—all directed and conditioned by the vast acquisition of wealth. Thus man has gradually lost the sense of resistance to temptation. In his primary desire for what he calls "happiness," which virtually is equated with personal ease and comfort, he has eagerly and abundantly accepted the gifts of Satan that stress earthly possessions, an almost total absence of concern for one's fellow men, and a concentration on this material life that embraces cars, drink, sexual abandonment, and a complete disdain for what cannot be evaluated in terms of money. And to the Devil, he says, with the rest. And the Devil, wise in the ways of men, readily accepts the challenge, for he has assumed dominion over the rest.

VIII

WOMAN: SATAN'S BAIT

THE MIDDLE AGES viewed the flesh, as represented by Woman, as impure and having been accursed since Eve. Woman was unclean. The flesh and the Devil were one. Woman is the Bride of Satan, and with Satan's cooperation she can lure men by offering her wares. She can revive spent passion. She can offer her lustful body to the inflamed excitements of men. Once an offer is accepted, the man is doomed. He is the bound slave of the woman. And by inference he is in the everlasting power of her master, the Fiend himself.

To the ecclesiastical mind of the Middle Ages, woman was the bane of mankind. Association with her was catastrophic. She ensnared men. She was the cat's-paw of Satan. The clerics in France in particular made no bones about it. They saw the Devil in woman's beauty. They called it The Devil in Woman.

Woman seduces man. She corrupts his morality, his sense of integrity, his honesty, his virtue. She tempts him away from righteousness. Housewives and high-born ladies are equally debauched and licentious, in varying degrees, and they readily debauch sober, upright men. By her nudity, her carnal attractions, she destroys burghers and princelings, youths and elders. She is the demoniac lust of the flesh.

Women have always presented a dichotomous nature. They are either passionately dedicated to religion, or equally devoted adherents of the Devil. This was a not unusual view of the medieval mind, for Satanic cults were merely a survival of religion, although largely of pagan religion. Thus witches and sorceresses have always been more numerous than their male counterparts—warlocks, necromancers, karcists, and all sorts of occultists.

Traditionally, women in obscure folklore and legends as well as among theologians, have been credited with Satanic coitus. The Devil, in human form, became the incubus, and the pliant and willing woman constituted the succubus. The resultant progeny was an abomination, bestial, nonhuman, malefic.

In classical antiquity woman presented an image compounded of evil, deceit, and wantonness. Euripides, the Greek dramatist, exclaims in *Hippolytus*:

Great Zeus, why didst thou, to man's sorrow, put woman, evil counterfeit, to dwell where shines the sun? . . . As soon as ever we would bring this plague into our home we bring its fortune to the ground. It is clear from this how great a curse a woman is; the very father, that begot and nurtured her, to rid him of the mischief, gives her a dower and packs her off; while the husband, who takes the noxious weed into his home, fondly decks his sorry idol in fine raiment.

Aristophanes, the Greek comedy writer, has the same attitude toward women. In *Lysistrata* the leader of the chorus says:

No wild beast is there, no flame or fire, more fierce and untamable than woman; the leopard is less savage and shameless.

Menander, another Greek comedy writer, cries, in the tones of the later medieval clerics:

Now may he perish, root and branch, who was the first to marry and then the second, and next the third, and then the fourth, and then the last one on the list.

Menander's words are re-echoed by the Church Father St. Jerome (c. 348–420):

Woman is the true Satan, the foe of peace, the source of impatience, the subject of dissension, whose absence brings assured tranquillity.

Clement of Alexandria (c. 150–c. 216), an earlier Church Father, had been equally condemnatory of any relations with women. His view was that base pleasure, even if experienced in marriage, was unjust. For base pleasure was the bait held out by Satan.

Tertullian, too, with misogynistic violence, fulminated against the sex:

Woman, you are the gateway of the devil. You persuaded him whom the devil dared not attack directly.

Again:

Woman is a temple built over a sewer.

Throughout the Middle Ages, female licentiousness was attributed by the Church to Satan's encouragement. In the sixteenth century, women and girls were attracted to an institute called the *Disciplina Gynopygica*. The founder was a Dutchman, Cornelius Andraenson, who subjected the women to perverted erotic practices.

Women have thus readily become aides of the Devil. They

have used their erotic charms and delectable ways in the service of the Lord of the Nether Regions. With their carnal weapons they are capable of annihilating man, body and soul. Satan endows them with occult powers. They can concoct potions that will destroy crops and cattle, or bring affection to lovesick suppliants, or drive men into maniacal frenzies. They perform obscene ceremonies and sacrifices to enlist the Devil's demons. They read the stars and foretell ominous events. They see portents in the heavens, in the constellations and in their conjunctions. They haunt graveyards and commune with dead spirits. They cast spells on those who oppose them. With their capacity for levitation, they can cover vast spaces in a flash of time. They thus have a wide and unhampered field for their activities, provided they give allegiance to the Satanic power. As queens and concubines, as harlots and chaste maidens, they have moved thrones and upheaved empires, in ancient Babylonia and in Byzantium, in the warring states of the European Continent, in manor and castle. Princelings and burghers, scholars and adventurers, poets and artists sell their soul for an embrace, a kiss, a promising glance from their eyes. "Make me immortal with a kiss," cries Faustus when he beholds Helen.

In the Middle Ages witches were the *good women*. This term was used in fear of their retaliation, just as in antiquity the Erinyes, the Furies, were euphemistically called Eumenides, the gracious goddesses. Paracelsus, in fact, the great sixteenth-century physician, alchemist, and occultist, cast aside the bookish wisdom stored in Hebrew, Latin, and Arabic treatises, and declared that the best medicine was that known to the witches, the *good women*.

These *good women* used in their practice comforters, *solanaceae*. These comforters were exotic vegetables, plants and herbs: love-apples, lady's fox-gloves and poison-queller (*vince venenum*), mandragore, bittersweet, and nightshade.

Many of the ingredients in the philtres were poisonous in themselves, but in conjunction with others might and could effect a cure for certain ailments. And the Middle Ages knew every ailment, particularly such as related to skin conditions. Hence the witches were consulted in time of need and urgency. For they had the power, the diabolic capacity, transmitted to them by the demons, to control nature, to wrest it to their purpose. So even if something beneficent was achieved, it retained the Satanic stigma.

These medieval women, by the very condition of their close confinement to domestic life, to labor in the fields, to submission to the lord of the manor and to their own marital partner, sought for an outlet to their energies and their undefined hopes. In many cases they tended to envision another way of life, closely allied to their inner meditations, their mental projection. They created fanciful images in which they were personally involved. They were led by hallucinations and delusory thoughts into strange possibilities. The dark flow of transmitted beliefs, ceremonials, legends, filled with potent deeds, with adventurous doings and unimagined audacities, struck sharply into their consciousness. Or, secluded and abandoned by the community, living in some remote spot by the shore, in some woodland, deep in the forest, they grew at one with the natural conditions surrounding them, with herbs and plants, trees and animals and the furry creatures of the undergrowth. And in their loneliness they adopted, as a makeshift for some human contact, a vole or toad, a stray mongrel, a lizard. Anything, any object that would give them a sense of belonging. And in their confused daydreams perhaps a sense of belonging closely, dynamically, with some superior, some encouraging and inspiring agent. In the scattered villages, many women longed to be participants in some stirring atmosphere, far removed from the bleak drabness of peasant toil.

Some of these women were of a natural simplicity of character. Some were driven, on the other hand, by perverse urgencies and, in the general and widespread climate of their surroundings, they saw about them the dark spirits, the shapeless elementals, the fiends who were the vanguard of the demoniac forces. They believed implicitly in Satan's potency. He changed people and brought hidden treasures into the open. He revealed the future. He destroyed hostile neighbors and helped his supporters at a price.

Under the aegis of the infernal hierarchy, these women crystallized and materialized their emotional compulsions. They might abandon home and husband and children, lover and parents. Their resolve was made. They had consummated their pact with the Evil One, and they saw that it was good. The cult of Satan was established in them. Obscene ceremonies were directed to the glorification of his majesty. Women rallied round their knight in dark armor. They formed squadrons for mutual interests and for support in an increased feeling of belonging to a powerful protective society. They convened in covens of twelve, with the Master as the thirteenth member. Diabolical rites were practiced at set times of the year. Occult feasts took place in segregated woodland spots. At certain times the Fiend himself honored them with his presence. For this purpose they came from remote regions, from the mountains and the river banks, from distant islands and forgotten haunts. And then the old pagan Greek and Roman, Syrian and Asian cults, stubbornly resistant in the middle centuries, culminated in a riotous febrile dionysiac release of all sexual restraint.

Now fully initiated, now experienced in the occult ways, a woman could ply her witchery masterfully. Man must be subdued, seduced, bent to her will. And Satan, in his cunning way, was ever at hand to offer women as bait to weak or passionate or prospectively subservient male neophytes.

So the influence of woman, in a sinister direction, was

pervasive throughout the courts and palaces of Europe, as well as in hovel and farmstead and hamlet. Women dabbled in the black arts, probing into astrology and its interpretations. They participated in abhorrent sacrificial rites. They recognized no barriers. They were intent on achieving their ends and gaining the approval of their Master. In the fifteenth century there was Eleanor Cobham, the wife of the Duke of Gloucester, who was charged with necromantic performances encouraged by the Satanic spirit. Two centuries later Eleanor Tuchet appeared. She lured men by professing divination with demoniac help. Stevenote de Audebert admitted in 1616 having made a pact with the Devil. There was Isabel Smith, and there was the Scottish witch, Agnes Sampson. And there were hosts of others, nameless but maleficent.

In France there were the notorious witches and practitioners in potions, Catherine La Voisin and Perrenon Megain. Marie Lamont, a noble Scottish lady, confessed herself a witch and admitted encounters with Satan. Lady Alice Kyteler was a witch who buried four husbands after poisoning them all. And did not the first man, Adam himself, consort, as Assyrian demonology and Talmudic tradition agree, with the female demon Lilith?

All these women, and many more in the long dark history of the Black Arts, practiced their skills, their secret occupations, in the name of the Devil. They proclaimed his aid. They hymned his ascendancy. They exulted in their conspiratorial intimacy with his final purpose of pursuing man and exercising the utmost penalties of body and soul on his very existence.

☙ IX ☙

THE SABBAT: THE BLACK MASS

PAGANISM AND Christianity had been in violent conflict in
the fourth and fifth centuries. And although Christianity
triumphed over its opponents, paganism did not disappear
completely. It went underground and remained so for long
centuries, still resistant, still exerting its influence. Ancient
rites, the arcana of priestly codes, mystic cults, retained
something of the antique dominance. Rejecting Christianity, then, as a newcomer intruding on its mysteries, paganism rallied its adherents and equipped them with weapons
against the enemy. And Satan, as the archenemy of Christianity, resumed his role as the commander of the opposing
hosts. He became the guardian of necromantic practices, of
consultations with fiendish spirits. He gathered his followers
from hut and cell, from the fields and the courts. He summoned his adventurers, his distorted souls, his lonely and
frustrated women. He became the apotheosis of the Magic
Arts, offering the key to power and domination and the released passions of men.

The blasphemous apotheosis of Satan appears in an ex-
traordinary, furtive ritual that was prevalent in many rural

areas in the Middle Ages. This ritual is known as the Sabbat, and the ceremony that was often associated with it is
called the Black Mass. The word *Sabbat* has been the subject of etymological dispute. Some writers take the word as
stemming from the Hebrew *Sabbath*, which would make the
Sabbat a travesty of the Judaic religion. Others propose that
the word is a derivative from the French verb *s'ébattre*, to
hold a revel.

The whole formidable mystery of the secret cults, of
magic rituals and astrological influences and computations
and Satanic forces, is summed up by the poet John Donne:

> Go, and catche a falling starre,
>   Get with child a mandrake root,
> Tell me, where all past years are,
>   Or who cleft the Devil's foot.

Descriptions of Sabbat ceremonies are to be found in the
confessions made by witches at their trials. And it is noteworthy that witches were always more numerous than sorcerers. One demonographer states that in the reign of the
French Louis XIII "for one sorcerer there are 10,000 sorceresses." Another demonographer confirmed this view: "We
should speak of the Heresy of the sorceresses, not of the
sorcerers. The latter are of little account."

In England and France, in Germany, Spain, and Italy, in
Salem and other towns of New England, young and old
women, under harsh interrogations accompanied by excruciating torture, admitted their glorification of the Infernal
Lord: admitted their blasphemies and stercoraceous and unnatural rituals. Sometimes they even confessed their extreme
pleasure in their acts, their sense of total involvement, their
utter Satanic devotion, and their belief in the omnipotence
and domination of the Fiend.

These confessions were extracted by investigators and inquisitors—both ecclesiastical and secular—lawyers, priests, civil authorities. They are incorporated in the accounts recorded by the medieval demonographers. Jean Bodin wrote on the subject in 1580, in his *Démonomanie des Sorciers.* Henri Boguet, a French jurist, published, a few decades later, his *Discours des Sorciers.* Martin Delrio, a sixteenth-century Spanish prosecutor, is the author of a monumental *Disquisitionum Magicarum Libri Sex,* published in Louvain in 1599. It is a corpus of diabolic techniques and practices. So too are Francesco Guazzo's *Compendium Maleficarum,* published in Milan in 1608, and Nicholas Remy's *Demonolatria,* published in 1595.

The most important of them all, possibly, for its influence and its extensive rules for detecting Satanic operations, was the *Malleus Maleficarum,* The Witches' Hammer. This was the work of two Dominicans, Heinrich Kramer and Jacob Sprenger. This book was the official text used by the Church in the investigation and punishment of witches.

The ritual itself is traditionally a survival from antiquity, from pagan cults, especially those that were prevalent in Syria, Persia, and the Mesopotamian region, where the Satanic spirit was considered a supreme force equal in power to the beneficent Divinity himself, and in fact beneficent to his votaries. The gradual evolution of Christian ceremonials, liturgies, and dogma banished the worship of the Devil. But not altogether so. Adherence to the diabolic agents did not disappear either immediately or completely. It survived, however furtively and precariously at first, with remarkable persistence in peasant areas, in remote valleys, on islands far from the coast, in mountainous country, in abandoned ruins where occasional wanderers congregated for some kind of contact: wherever, in fact, Christian influence was able to penetrate only slowly and with difficulty. One such notorious haunt was the mountain of the Bructeri, in Germany. Others were in Swedish forests, in lonely French countrysides, in the sweeping expanses along the banks of the Danube, on Mt. Tonale in the Eastern Alps, on Mt. Vaskapu in Hungary.

Witches came from distant hamlets and mountains, from towns and islands and valleys, from crofts and farmsteads to make obeisance and do honor to their master. Among notable assemblies were those held at Le Puys-de-dôme in France; in Spain, on the Sands of Seville; in Italy, on Mt. Paterno; in Iceland on the volcanic Mt. Hekla; in Germany, on the Horselberg and the Blocksberg. Even in Ceylon, every Saturday night all demons were said to attend an assembly called Yaksa Sabawa, The Witches' Sabbat.

The occult practices, those vestiges of what was known as the "old religion," were always in conflict and opposition with regard to Christian thought and belief. Hence they were essentially evil and ruinous. They were the forbidden Black Arts that the Bible called abominations. They were steeped in barbarous customs, tainted with the ghoulish acts of Hell's hosts. These practices manifested themselves at the Sabbat, and at the Black Mass.

The Sabbat reunion consisted of Satan's followers. They were magic-working crones and younger devotees as well, who conceived themselves as ministrants of the Devil or were branded by local talk as his satellites. Usually they met at night, as befitted the Fiend's tenebrous ways. Or, perversely, on Good Friday, at Meltane, which was Midsummer; at Roodmass, which was May Eve; or at Hallowmass. In contempt for Christian sacred days, they even met on Ascension Day, Holy Thursday, or St. John's Day.

Only the votaries and initiates of the Fiend participated in the ceremony. At the head was a young priestess known as The Ancient One. From accounts of various demonologists, we can form a fairly clear image of what occurred at these gatherings. There were, in this connection, widespread whispered hints and even positive assertions that acts of cannibalism, in which young children were the ritualistic victims, were not unknown.

Groups of witches convened in covens. A coven, a term which is a corruption of convent, consisted of twelve members. The thirteenth, the leader, was known as the Devil. The number thirteen itself was significant, being associated with the ancient lunar months. The moon, in fact, in antique pagan cults was presided over by the triple goddess Hecate. She had domain in the Lower Regions, where she throned it over the Black Arts.

In preparation for the ceremony, the witches anointed themselves. To create the sensation of levitation, it was said that they used belladonna. Riding their broomsticks through the scudding clouds of night, or astride a goat, a pig, a bear, a bat, or other creature that acted as a familiar, the occult adepts, says a medieval demonographer, advanced howling through the air, over the waters, borne by the wind, to do homage to their Mistress Gulifora, Queen of the Sabbat. One chronicler stated that some witches went on foot, accompanied by their children. But on the return journey they carried these children home through the air.

There was no compunction, no indecision about the purpose of the macabre gathering. The priestess opened the hideous proceedings with the words: I will come to the altar. Save me, Lord Satan, from the treacherous and the violent.

As a travesty of the old Christian *agape,* the love feast, a meal was prepared that was obscene in appearance and nauseating to the taste. A shaggy goat was sacrificed to the Devil, who too appeared in goat likeness. After shrieking demoniac invocations, the Sabbat culminated in more sacrificial offerings, in lewd dance rituals. The dance was invariably *widdershins,* that is, from west to east, in opposition to the motion of the sun. *Widdershins* was a movement always associated with occult rites, because by its unnatural direction it was in harmony with evil energies.

The Devil was honored with the *osculum obscaenum,* the obscene kiss on his hindquarters. Then followed brutal sexual promiscuities, during which it was believed that the witches had carnal intercourse with the Demon.

In a trancelike state, often induced by drugs, the witches could be hypnotically responsive to visions and spectacles that had been mentally projected into a kind of objective reality. And the result was that reality and thought-forms merged into an undefined unity.

In this obfuscated condition, the witches indulged in all kinds of scatological obscenities. They reveled in human filth. They reeked of pus and excrement and bodily fluids. They did not wash and thus felt closer to the characteristic attribute of the Prince of Stenches himself. And all their rituals and their bacchanalian revelry took place under cover of the night.

For light was inimical to all occult practices. And at the first glimmer of dawn, at the crowing of the cock, the nocturnal and infernal assembly vanished.

Strange testimony, offered by staid chroniclers as well as fanatical prosecutors of magic performers and accused women, has been given in the course of the ages with respect to the actuality of the Sabbat conventions.

In the fourteenth century an altar was dedicated to Him who had been Wronged. Among the assemblage of women was a Devil's Bride. She had to be at least thirty years of age, says a demonographer. She must be beautiful, with tragic eyes and long snaky tresses. On her head she wore a crown of vervain.

There was dancing, known as the Sabbat-round. It was a strange, hieratic form of stylized movements. The dancers were back to back, their arms behind them. They often touched each other's back, but without seeing each other.

Later in the evening, a woman would become the altar itself. Prostrate, with her hair in the dust and soil, she lay naked. On her back, a demon officiated. Prayers were said, backward. Then came a pledge of love, a cake baked on the woman's body. Lastly, there were two offerings—one of the most recently dead, the other of the most recently born in the district.

Women brought a toad, dressed up, and pulled it to pieces. Then, raising their eyes to heaven, the women would each behead a toad. In derision, Jesus was invoked as John or Jack, the usual medieval term used by the Satan-worshipers.

A remarkable account of the Sabbat and its participants is related in Conway's *Demonology*, published in the 1870's. It runs as follows:

In 1669 the people of the villages of Mohra and Elfdale in Sweden, believing that they were troubled by witches, were visited by a royal commission, the result of whose investigations was the execution of twenty-three adults and fifteen children; running of the gauntlet by thirty-six between the ages of nine and sixteen years; the lashing on the hand of twenty children for three Sundays at the church-door, and similar lashing of the aforesaid thirty-six once a week for a year. Portions of the confessions of the witches are given below from the Public Register as translated by Anthony Horneck, D.D., and printed in London, anno 1700. I add a few words in brackets to point out survivals.

"We of the province of Elfdale do confess that we used to go to a gravel-pit which lay hard by a cross-way [Hecate], and there we put on a vest [Wolf-girdle] over our heads, and then danced round, and after this ran to the cross-way, and called the Devil thrice, first with a still voice, the second time somewhat louder, and the third time very loud, with these words—*Antecessor, come and carry us to Blockula.* Whereupon immediately he used to appear, but in different habits; but for the most part we saw him in a grey coat and red and blue stockings: he had a red beard [Barbarossa], a high-crowned hat [Turncap], with linen of divers colours wrapt about it, and long garters upon his stockings.

"Then he asked us whether we would serve him with soul and

body. If we were content to do so, he set us upon a beast which he had there ready, and carried us over churches and high walls; and after all we came to a green meadow where Blockula lies. We must procure some scrapings of altars, and filings of church clocks; and then he gives us a horn with a salve in it, wherewith we do anoint ourselves [chrism]; and a saddle with a hammer [Thor's], and a wooden nail, thereby to fix the saddle [Walkyr's]; whereupon we call upon the Devil and away we go.

"For their journey, they said they made use of all sorts of instruments, of beasts, of men, of spits, and posts, according as they had opportunity: if they do ride upon goats [Azazel] and have many children with them, that all may have room, they stick a spit into the backside of the Goat, and then are anointed with the aforesaid ointment. What the manner of their journey is, God only knows. Thus much was made out, that if the children did at any time name the names [Egyptian spells] of those that had carried them away, they were again carried by force either to Blockula, or to the cross-way, and there miserably beaten, insomuch that some of them died of it.

"A little girl of Elfdale confessed that, naming the name of JESUS as she was carried away, she fell suddenly upon the ground, and got a great hole in her side, which the Devil presently healed up again, and away he carried her; and to this day the girl confessed she had exceeding great pain in her side.

"They unanimously confessed that Blockula is situated in a delicate large meadow, whereof you can see no end. The place or house they met at had before it a gate painted with divers colours; through this gate they went into a little meadow distinct from the other, where the beasts went that they used to ride on; but the men whom they made use of in their journey stood in the house by the gate in a slumbering posture, sleeping against the wall [castle of Waldemar]. In a huge large room of this house, they said, there stood a very long table, at which the witches did sit down; and that hard by this room was another chamber where there were very lovely and delicate beds. The first thing they must do at Blockula was, that they must deny all, and devote themselves body and soul to the Devil, and promise to serve him faithfully, and confirm all this with an oath [initiation]. Hereupon they cut their fingers [Odinism], and with their blood write their name in his book [Revelations]. They added that he caused them to be baptized, too, by such priests as he had there [Antichrist's Sacraments].

"And he, the Devil, bids them believe that the day of judgment will come speedily, and therefore sets them on work to build a great house of stone [Babel], promising that in that house he will preserve them from God's fury, and cause them to enjoy the greatest delights and pleasures [Moslem]. But while they work exceeding hard at it, there falls a great part of the wall down again.

"They said, they had seen sometimes a very great Devil like a Dragon, with fire round about him, and bound with an iron chain [Apocalyptic], and the Devil that converses with them tells them that if they confess anything he will let that great Devil loose upon them, whereby all Sweedeland shall come into great danger.

"They added that the Devil had a church there, such another as in the town of Mohra. When the Commissioners were coming he told the Witches they should not fear them; for he would certainly kill them all. And they confessed that some of them had attempted to murther the Commissioners, but had not been able to effect it.

"Some of the children talked much of a white Angel [Frigga as Christian tutelary], which used to forbid them what the Devil had bid them do, and told them that those doings should not last long. What had been done had been permitted because of the wickedness of the people.

"Those of Elfdale confessed that the Devil used to play upon an harp before them [Tannhauser], and afterwards to go with them that he liked best into a chamber, when he committed venerous acts with them [Asmodeus]; and this indeed all confessed, that he had carnal knowledge of them, and that the Devil had sons and daughters by them, which he did marry together, and they . . . brought forth toads and serpents [Echidna].

"After this they sat down to table, and those that the Devil esteemed most were placed nearest to him; but the children must stand at the door, where he himself gives them meat and drink

[Sacrament]. After meals they went to dancing, and in the meanwhile swore and cursed most dreadfully, and afterwards went to fighting one with another [Valhalla].

"They also confessed that the Devil gives them a beast about the bigness and shape of a young cat [Hecate], which they call a carrier; and that he gives them a bird as big as a raven [Odin's messenger], but white; and these two creatures they can send anywhere, and wherever they come they take away all sorts of victuals they can get, butter, cheese, milk, bacon, and all sorts of seeds, whatever they find, and carry it to the witch. What the bird brings they may keep for themselves, but what the carrier brings they must reserve for the Devil, and that is brought to Blockula, where he doth give them of it so much as he thinks fit. They added likewise that these carriers fill themselves so full sometimes, that they are forced to spue ['Odin's booty'] by the way, which spuing is found in several gardens, where colworts grow, and not far from the houses of these witches. It is of a yellow colour like gold, and is called butter of witches.

"The Lords Commissioners were indeed very earnest, and took great pains to persuade them to show some of their tricks, but to no purpose; for they did all unanimously confess that since they had confessed all, they found that all their witchcraft was gone, and that the Devil at this time appeared to them very terrible, with claws on his hands and feet, and with horns on his head, a long tail behind, and showed to them a pit burning, with a hand put out; but the Devil did thrust the person down again with an iron fork; and suggested to the witches that if they continued in their confession, he would deal with them in the same manner."

The ministers of both Elfdale and Mohra were the chief inciters of this investigation, and both testified that they had suffered many tortures in the night from the witches. One was taken by the throat and so violently used that "for some weeks he was not able to speak or perform divine service."

The Black Mass too has historical confirmation. The usual view on its origin is that the Sabbat springs from pagan rites, while the Black Mass is a deliberate sacrilegious distortion of Christian ceremonies. In its salacious liturgy, its inverted lewd rites, it is a flagrant, manifest demonstration against Christian faith and doctrine. It sets Satan on a pinnacle as the Supreme Ruler of the Infernal Powers, embracing all the secretive and malign forces that pervade the cosmos.

Centuries later, the Black Mass acquired a ritualistic importance of its own and was celebrated without reference to the Sabbat. Those who participated in these Black Rites were not necessarily witches or professional warlocks. But in their perverted ways they displayed an intense and unholy interest in the unedifying procedures that marked the Black Mass. Unfrocked and lewd priests, ignorant rustics, scholars, polished but wayward ladies of the European courts, dabblers in the occult, and adventurers were in varying degrees drawn to the barbarous and brutal features that made the Black Mass a monstrosity in the history of human culture.

Once the Christian Mass with its ritual was used by magicians as a potent means of effecting their operations. In the medieval grimoires such as The Red Dragon, The Grimoire of Honorius, The Testament of Solomon, the Red Book of Appin, there were special incantations and conjurations and passages taken from the Mass but distorted perversely for occult reasons.

The Christian Mass became the Black Mass, Satan's own ritual. It celebrated the Devil, and consequently the phraseology used was a categorical negation of Christian views and rejected the context and the contents of the orthodox Mass. Black was the keynote in a spectacle that testified to a bitter hatred of Christianity. Black hosts were used. Chalices were black in color. Perverted or unfrocked priests and equally licentious nuns performed the foulest variations of sexual aberrations. Human flesh was part of the unhallowed banquets. Girls appeared naked, sharing in the ritual. It was a spectacle that seemed like the source of the Marquis de Sade's descriptions of monstrous feasts.

Beelzebub was in the ascendant. Hosannas were proclaimed in his name. And the Devil himself, repeat the old demonologists, was present as chief officiant. Altogether it was a sacrilegious burlesque, but it had sinister features, and it was a salacious orgiastic demonstration.

This glorification of Satan as the Antichrist was particularly in vogue in France, in the latter decades of the seventeenth century. Official cognizance was taken, however, and many priests and other participants in the black rites were convicted, imprisoned, or executed.

Such Satanic Masses are by no means unknown even in these days. Satanism and its expression in the Black Mass and kindred rites occur in London, in Paris, in Rome, and in England—in short, wherever sophistication, exhausted by novelties, seeks yet another amelioration of its boredom.

A stark description of the Black Mass appears in *Là-Bas* —Down There—by the French novelist Joris Karl Huysmans. This book, published in 1891, purports to be a personal account, seen through the eyes of the principal character Durtal, of Satanic rites. Durtal is conducted to a chapel where, in a misty, pungent atmosphere created by the burning of nightshade and myrtle, rue and henbane, he observes blasphemous and diabolic spectacles in which Christian ceremonial and liturgy are outraged and defiled. A Mass is said by an infamous priest who, under his red chasuble, stands naked. A Satanic touch is added by his cap, adorned with two red horns fashioned of cloth. The acolytes, chanting in a choir, are homosexuals. The presiding priest invokes the Devil, lauding and eulogizing him for his defilements, his crimes, his vices, and his furious opposition to Christianity. During these pronouncements rise the shrieks of the approving congregation. And the climax is reached in the usual orgiastic license.

Captain John Smith, the colonizer of Virginia in 1607, describes the aborigines of Virginia as Devil-worshipers who sacrificed children to Oke (Satan). Similar practices were prevalent in both North and South America, as well as in neighboring islands. In Florida, native tribes worshiped Toia, the Bad Spirit. Inhabitants of Haiti performed demonolatrous ceremonies: dancing and prancing in circular procession around a figure that was horned and snake-entwined and surrounded by animal-headed half-human forms upholding pitchforks.

The principal element in the Black Mass is the epiphany of Satan himself. He stands attended imperially by his baleful legions. These polymorphous creatures resemble the shadowy but still visible hosts of hell that Cellini describes in his autobiography. In the medieval centuries Satan is represented in his ebony black skin, with horned head. He is cloven-hoofed, while from his gaping mouth fiery flames spurt and writhe.

Sometimes the Satanic image is feline or canine. But most frequently he manifests himself in hircine form. At times too he was known, especially by the Neoplatonic philosophers such as Plotinus and Porphyry, as a monstrous five-shaped figure, a Pentamorph.

In Travancore, India, it is said that the Evil Power approaches in the form of a dog, as Mephistopheles approached Faust.

The Black Mass might be celebrated in some dark crypt, secluded in its horrifying rites. Cloisters, too, or a deserted chapel might be chosen, as a cynical and profane gesture that defied orthodoxy. There the participants who craved the foul excitement made obeisance to the diabolic figure. They invoked him and then set about the performance of their grim rites. In the dark confinement, calling upon their Master, they released their passions in a vortex of sensual delirium and turned the final phase of the ritual into aphrodisiac contortions.

The Black Mass appealed to the highly sophisticated, to the wealthy and idle society that had experienced every normal entertainment. This society clamored for something fresh and untried in the way of diversion. It was ready for every contingency, every mollification of a vapid life, or every adventure spiced with danger in any form, physical or spiritual. In the seventeenth century the French court was a focal point for such experiences. Historically, there is detailed evidence of some of the demoniac ceremonials that were prevalent during this period. Madame de Montespan, the notorious mistress of King Louis XIV, was the principal figure in one particular Black Mass. Fearing the loss of the king's interest in her, she enlisted the services of a certain Catherine La Voisin, reputed to be an adept in magic and in concocting love potions. With the help of the unscrupulous Abbé Guibourg, Black Mass performances were staged. The priestly officiants were lavishly robed. Drink was spiced with aphrodisiacs. The Fiend was invoked in a kabalistic conjuration. Madame de Montespan herself, stripped of all her clothes, took part in a rite in which, under cover of clouds of incense and mystic chants, children were immolated to his Infernal Majesty. As usual, the climax was a febrile promiscuous sexual convulsion.

Sometimes the Black Mass was performed on a girl's nude body. Black tapers, burning low, added to the horror of the macabre scene, while the blood of a sacrificed child was proffered to Satan as Asmodeus and to Atargatis, who is also Astoreth, the Asian goddess of sexual lust.

A notorious character in this respect was Gilles de Rais (c. 1404–1440), once Marshal of France. In the course of a brief but turbulent life, he had gained a revolting reputation. He was an adventurer, a murderer, a patron of literature, a Satanist. In the days of his vast prosperity he had maintained a luxurious court. When his fortune ebbed away, he attached himself to Francesco Prelati, a Florentine priest who was also a sorcerer. Prelati encouraged and helped De Rais to regain his fortune by means of the occult arts. He turned to necromancy, alchemy, and Satanism. He showed fiendish zest and brutality and a total lack of any moral sense in exploiting his acquired skills. He was involved in the ritual murder of children whom he had kidnaped for his purpose. In the result, he was hanged, but his notoriety still stains the Satanic and historical chronicles.

The eighteenth century was equally notorious. It fostered secret clubs, such as the Mollies and the Beaux, that were popular in London and elsewhere. The members were mostly wealthy sportsmen or men about town. They were known as Mohawks and Sons of Midnight. Free of all scruples, they searched assiduously for new sensations to arouse their jaded bodies and minds. They found such experiences in performing, in private and country estates, Satanic rites that included the Black Mass. One of the most repulsive and most vicious of such coteries was called the Hell Fire Club, or the Friars of Medmenham. The guiding spirit and leader was a wealthy, degenerate esthete named Sir Francis Dashwood.

Dashwood had traveled widely on the Continent and had acquired occult skills and Satanic knowledge. In England he set up his Club in the ruins of Medmenham Abbey, in Buckinghamshire. The year was 1750. The Abbey was furnished by him with expensive lavishness. Lascivious frescoes and engravings adorned the walls. Chambermaids and women guests were dressed as nuns, in flimsy and alluring robes to whet the appetites of the clubmen. The members themselves were robed as monks. The essential purpose of the Club was to parody, with irreligious barbarity and lewdness, the rites and the liturgies of the Christian Church. Virtually, the Club was an elaborate private brothel where the Black Mass was performed by the president of the Club. As was customary in such rites, the concluding feature ended in sexual riotousness. Oddly, the Abbey permitted no clock on the premises. Evidently it was thought that in the circumstances the measurement of time was both useless and meaningless. The abominations, consequently, were unconfined. The cells of the Abbey were used for every type of erotic perversion until the scandal reached such a height that the performances were stopped.

It is worth noting that Dashwood himself belonged to the English aristocracy, as did other members of the Club. Dashwood was actually Chancellor of the Exchequer. Among the other members, one became the Prime Minister, and another was chosen as the Lord Mayor of London.

The Satanic rituals had now reached their climax. The members of the Hell Fire Club, literate and amoral, fell to the level of the bewildered old beldames and the perplexed creatures who found in the diabolic rites an enthralling vista of personal power and achievement.

Reversing Christian ritual, the Black Mass imitated the sacraments and performed a Last Supper of its own, while the host was called White John. A lamb was sometimes offered to Lucifer, to the accompaniment of a blessing: that the Peace of Lucifer might reign over the victim. One demonographer describes how the officiant, robed in black, turns his back to the altar and elevates a black turnip, intoning a prayer meanwhile asking the Master to help all witches.

In the case of a human sacrifice, Astorath and Asmodeus were invoked. Let them accept, ran the conjuration, the offering in return for granting the wishes of the suppliant. Vows, incantations, supplications, the Pater Noster were all recited backward, so that the entire retroverse procedure attacked and rejected religious orthodoxy.

X

DEVILISH EXPRESSIONS

THE DEVIL has intruded into men's minds and actions, into their decisions and involvements, into their intellectual and spiritual life. But he has gone further. He has attached himself in the most intimate sense to men's speech and talk. He has wrapped himself round the human tongue, so that our conversation pours out a stream of exclamations, proverbs, and explanations that demonstrate Satan's participation in man's power of expression.

Every language contains the Satanic stamp, his diabolical idiom. In the English language alone, he is particularly manifest. This is especially true on the colloquial level, but no less so in other directions, in many fields of knowledge, in the scientific idiom, in legal phraseology, in the social means of communication.

We discuss an absent acquaintance and suddenly he appears before us, as if secretly summoned. In a tone that hints at some undefined but mysterious coincidence, we exclaim: *Talk of the devil!*

Nonchalance assumes a disregard for the externals—an indifference to other men and other circumstances. We describe a person so conditioned as a *devil-may-care* fellow.

Yet there are moments when Satan takes on an urbane politeness. Shakespeare in *King Lear* remarks that *the devil is a gentleman*—an opinion confirmed by Shelley in *Peter Bell the Third*.

The Devil is always in search of allies, and idlers are his ready victims.

For Satan finds some mischief still for idle hands to do, said Isaac Watts, the eighteenth-century theologian and hymnologist in *Against Idleness*.

Satan may not consistently display utter ruthlessness. He may reveal some innocuous trait, and human beings may then concede that his acts are without malice or injury. *Give the devil his due,* exclaims Cervantes, but, of course, there is a touch of irony in the injunction. The expression is also well illustrated in Shakespeare:

Jack, how agrees the devil and thee about thy soul, that thou soldest him on Good Friday last, for a cup of Madeira and cold capon's leg?

PRINCE: Sir John stands to his word, the devil shall have his bargain; for he was never yet a breaker of proverbs, he will give the devil his due.

—I HENRY IV, I.2

There is an old medieval Latin proverb that indicates Satan's wiliness. In its anonymous English rendering, it runs thus:

> The Devil was sick,
> The Devil a monk would be.
> The Devil was well,
> The Devil a monk was he.

On the other hand, the Fiend's acumen is traditionally belittled. Like the law, he is considered an ass. In *The Devil Is an Ass,* Ben Jonson so declares:

The devil is an ass, I do acknowledge it.

But there may be hidden virtues in him and he may not be totally malefic. The Elizabethan playwright Thomas Lodge says of him in *A Margarite of America:*

Devils are not so black as they are painted.

Retributions cannot be shirked, and Nemesis is always sure to punish the evildoer. That is folklore knowledge, and the thought has been incorporated into normal conversation. "Here's the devil to pay," exclaims Cervantes. And the devil is prompt in exacting payment. Traditionally, this expression has magic implications. A witch or sorcerer, operating with the devil's aid, was ultimately bound to give the devil his due payment.

The life of Sir Richard Burton, the English explorer and anthropologist, was a continuous restless disruption. He admitted that sometimes he could not explain his urgent wanderlust. The devil drives, he concluded. But long ago Rabelais had expressed the common, widespread idea of some compulsive action: "Needs must when the Devil drives."

It is to be noted that identical views on the Devil and his ways appear in many languages, first of all in the common speech, then imprinted in literary records. The linguistic expression may vary according to country or region, but the essential thought is remarkably the same.

Speed and efficiency in executing any plan are reasonable requirements. But dilatoriness is more than merely condemned: It is a Satanic threat as well, for the Evil One is on the watch for the laggard. The thought is crystallized in Beaumont and Fletcher's Elizabethan drama *Philaster:*

The Devil take the hindmost.

But drama, of course, merely repeats words and thoughts that have long been current in daily speech.

There is another, more picturesque explanation of this phrase. The reference is to a school of magic at Toledo in Spain. There were three such schools in the Middle Ages: at Toledo, at Salamanca, and at Cracow. To complete their academic course, students had to run through an underground passage. The last man, before reaching the exit, was assumed to be caught by the Devil and forced to become a Satanic imp.

Deceit and falsehood are among Satan's primary characteristics. Hence the truth will rout or humiliate him. In Part I, *King Henry IV*, Shakespeare produces the proverbial expression:

While you live, tell truth and shame the Devil.

The Common Prayer Book goes even further with its exhortation:

Renounce the Devil and all his works.

Satan has such a prolific progeny, so many offshoots of evil, that even mischievous youngsters are tarred with Satanic origins. So the expression *a limb of Satan* was long in vogue, brought into more prominence possibly by Mark Twain.

Satan's appearance is common knowledge: horns and tail and all. But there was an old legend that touched on the color of his tail. John Ruskin, in the *Architectural Magazine*, alludes to it:

The admiration of the "neat but not gaudy," which is commonly reported to have influenced the Devil when he painted his tail pea-green.

The phrase *the Devil's advocate* now implies a defense or plea on the wrong side of a case. Originally, it was applied to a person who argued against the canonization of a prospective saint.

In a general sense, whoever is inordinately cunning or destructive or ruthless or bestial is designated as a devil. Yet, in some perverse way, to be a *devil of a fellow* is almost a complimentary term, implying a sport, a jolly kind of adventurous man about town.

A *printer's devil* is a printer's errand boy who makes himself generally useful—a potential imp of mischief, capable of getting up to all sorts of pranks.

To devil, a culinary term, is evidently reminiscent of the fires of hell; but it means to grill meat with hot spices.

To assist a lawyer is to *devil for him.* Evidently the Fiend has a number of secondary functions in which he is ostensibly helpful.

But there is something sinister in the expression *to beat the devil's tattoo.* This is done by drumming with the fingers on a table or similar surface, to denote irritation or impatience. For Satan himself was always forthright, and would tolerate no hesitation.

In World War I the Scottish Highlanders were known to the enemy, for their abandon and aggressive courage, as the Ladies from Hell. In a somewhat similar sense, the Devil's Own was the name given to the 88th Foot, the Devil's Own Connaught Boys.

There is a religious inhibition in calling playing cards the *Devil's books,* as Swift called them.

In the early nineteenth century, the textile industry in England used machinery known as a *devil,* while the resultant cloth was called *devil's dust.*

What the devil has lost all sinister connotation. It is now just a sharp exclamation denoting surprise or impatience.

Putting salt on the devil's tail suggests the fiend's elusiveness as well as the impossibility of completing a task.

To play the devil is simply to act in an irrational manner.

The devil among the tailors is a picturesque way of describing a violent fracas.

Many plants, insects, and flowers have a diabolical appellation attached to them. These names are popularly used, and have no relation to the formal botanical terminology. The *devil-shrieker* is a tropical species of tree. *Devilwort* is a plant. The name given to a certain black beetle is *devil's cow*. The dragonfly is the *devil's needle*. Such folk names are neat and remarkably descriptive. A type of prickly pear is the *devil's fig*. A kind of prickly nettle becomes the *devil's leaf*. A certain plant whose stem strangles other plants is appropriately termed the *devil's guts*. The sun-spurge and similar plants that produce a milky juice are called *devil's milk*. A particular herb is known as the *devil's Bit*.

In nautical idiom, a split hook that grasps a cable link is a *devil's claw*.

In the British Isles and elsewhere, various locations, ravines, and bays have reputedly associations with Satan. There is a Devil's Den, a Devil's Punch Bowl, the Devil's Throat, the Devil's Stone, the Devil's Mill, the Devil's Dyke, the Devil's Hole. Presumably such names imply the work of the devil, or a fiendish haunt, or a hazard and danger to human beings. In the Zetland Islands two caverns are called the Devil's Nostrils. In Germany a stone, believed to cover a treasure, is known as the Devil's Altar.

The English classical scholar Richard Porson, whose life ended in far from academic associations, was known as Devil Dick. The eighteenth-century French sailor Jean Bart was called the French Devil for his intrepidity.

Voltaire's nickname was the Devil's Missionary. In Italy, in the thirteenth century, Ezzelino, the Ghibelline leader notorious for his cruelties, was termed *son of the devil*.

Vittoria Corombona, an Italian murderess, was known as *The White Devil.*

A hypocritical preacher is a *devil dodger.*

Lesage's novel *Le Diable Boiteux*—The Limping Devil —was known under its English title as *The Devil on Two Sticks.*

That strange plant the mandrake was called *devil's apple.* The Arabs name it the *devil's candle* from its shining appearance at night. The yellow bunting, that utters its note *deil,* was known in Scotland as the *devil's bird, deil* being the common term for devil. Dice, the game that often leads to ruin, is called the *devil's bones.*

A certain large beetle is described as the *devil's coach-horse.* The corn crowfoot similarly has vehicular associations. It is the *devil's coach-wheel.*

A shrewish woman, a termagant, must have something devilish in her composition. Naturally, she is the *devil's daughter.*

Numbers have, since the time of the ancient Greek mathematicians and especially Pythagoras, acquired mystic implications, occult symbolisms. Hence the number thirteen is the *Devil's dozen:* twelve forming a coven of witches, and the thirteenth member being Satan himself.

The innocuous game of whist has its diabolic touch. It is the *devil's four-poster.*

Black and yellow colors are the *devil's livery.* Black denotes death; yellow represents quarantine and sickness.

Extremely lucky persons were believed to have helpful but furtive contacts with Satan. Hence the expression *devil's luck.*

The English Parliament held in Coventry in 1459 to impeach the Yorkist leaders in the Wars of the Roses was termed the *Devil's Parliament.*

A puff-ball, which is a fungus full of dust, is whimsically known as the *devil's snuff-box.*

The common tongue, the popular speech, is always ingeniously prepared, with its picturesque talent for description, to pinpoint an object, a thought, a gesture, and to attach some fanciful relationship with Satan's multiform ways.

The devil's meal runs half to bran is a figurative way of indicating that what the devil does is far different from what he promises.

What does the devil eat? What are his tastes? We know in one instance that he is fond of mushrooms. In Portugal, pão do demonio, the devil's bread, is the term popularly used for mushrooms.

The Council of the Treasury is an august body, but it is known as the *Attorney-General's devils.*

As the devil loves holy water is virtually a strong negative, meaning not at all, for water drives away the fiend.

Between the devil and the deep sea implies between two hazards. The reference is to the herd of swine and devils called Legion in *Luke* 8:30.

Doing evil for profit, and giving some of the profit to the church is a way of *cheating the devil.*

He hath need of a long spoon that eateth with devil.

The suggestion is that you need your wits when dealing with the devil. In *The Tempest* we have:

Mercy! Mercy! this is a devil. I will leave him, I have no long spoon.

Pull devil, pull baker. Whether you lie or cheat, it is equally bad. In *Old Mortality,* Chapter 28, Walter Scott has, "Like Punch and the Deevil ragging about the Baker at the fair."

Something even worse than Satan is hinted at in the phrase the *devil and his dam,* that is, his wife.

It was thought that Ireland was besmirched in the expression *The Devil in Dublin City*. It was a scandalous notion. But the phrase is the result of philological confusion, for *Dublin* in Scandinavian is *Divelin*.

Much ado about nothing becomes, in Satanic phraseology, *the devil rides on a fiddlestick*. The expression occurs in Shakespeare, *I Henry IV*, ii, 4:

Heigh, heigh! the devil rides upon a fiddlestick: what's the matter?

In old churches there is a small door called a *devil's door*. It was opened during communion "to let the devil out." The north wall was called "the devil's side," because the Fiend and his demons haunted this spot to seize the unwary.

If you *kindle a fire for the devil*, you do something sinful with the impression of performing a devout act.

To hold a candle to the devil is to participate in evil activity. The allusion is to burning candles before the images of saints. Hence the reverse idea, of burning a candle to his Satanic Majesty.

To say the devil's paternoster is to grumble and to inveigh against fate.

In Yorkshire there are large stones called Druid stones. Their popular name is *devil's arrows*.

The current in the Bosporus, notorious for its great velocity, is known as the *devil's current*. Among the hills of Dumfrieshire, in the south of Scotland, there is a large hollow called *The Devil's Beeftub*. The tradition is that formerly raiders at the Border used to hide their stolen cattle there.

In Cornwall there is a tin mine, once operated by the Romans, that is now called the *devil's frying-pan*.

Different nations—different regions—each have their own view of the Devil, their own peculiar idiom to express the fiend's nature and his operations.

The Cornish folk say: He hates him as the Devil hates holy water.

Behind the cross stands the Devil is an ominous Spanish saying.

A Russian proverb runs: The Devil said he had all the kingdoms of the world; but God refused him even the rule of the swine.

The notion of the sense of family kinship, in an evil sense, is pithily interpreted in the Scottish expression: The De'il's aye good to his ain.

Germany says: There is no head so holy but that the Devil does not make a nest of it. Or: The Devil is master of all arts.

Avarice is particularly condemned in: The Devil lies brooding in the miser's chest.

And again: The Devil catches most souls in a golden net.

In a general sense, objects that have unusual features, ideas that contain some sinister or harmful implication, are not unreasonably linked with a diabolical origin or relationship.

The following lines by Daniel Defoe have a cynical, realistic turn:

> Wherever man erects a house of prayer
> The devil always builds a chapel there,
> And 'twill be found upon examination
> The latter has the larger congregation.

Moslems, noted for their total reliance on Kismet, laud the leisurely ways. Haste is from Satan, they say.

A commentary on the gourmandizing habits of the medieval monastic Orders dwells spicily on this custom: God sent the abbeys, but the Devil sent the kitchens and the cellars.

A French adage, which has its counterpart in Spanish, is a warning: When the Devil says his *Pater noster,* he means to cheat you.

One may understand like an angel, declares an anonymous apothegm, and yet be a Devil.

This Italian proverb is wry: The Devil tempts all, but the idle man tempts the Devil.

In Scotland a husband overwhelmed by a wife's nagging sent her to the Evil One. A Scottish song made this situation the theme of a song:

Ye've heard how the de'il, as he wanchel'd through Beith
Wi' a wife in ilk oxter, an' ane in his teeth,
When some ane cried oot, "Will you tak' mine the morn?"
He wagged his auld tail while he cocket his horn,
   But only said, "Im-hm,"
Wi' sic a big mouthfu' he couldna say A-y-e.

Lucifer at one time must have been considered a pillar of the Church, for the calendar of the Church includes St. Lucifer.

An old saying belonging to the days of sailing ships runs: The Devil to pay and no pitch hot.

In this context, the Devil is a seam between the garboard-strake and the peel in the old wooden ships. To pay meant to cover it with pitch. The pitch had to be ready, as the ship was careened between the tides.

⚔ XI ⚔

SOME SATANIC CHARACTERS

To THE Satanist, the Archfiend, the fallen angel, the victim
of the divine wrath, is not evil. He is not a violent, destructive enemy of mankind. On the contrary, he has been ma-
ligned, since Biblical times on through the middle centuries down to the present. Admittedly, he is a rebel, but
he is a titanic, heroic rebel, as Milton depicted him. He is
of the stature of Prometheus, also a rebel against supreme
authority—and tyranny.

To the adherents of Satan he is the primal victim of the
Supreme Agent, and hence becomes a sympathetic figure who
evokes compassion, then reverence and awe and adoration.
For the Satanist consistently looks upon the Fiend as a benefactor of mankind—ill-treated once, but without bitter resentments, and always powerful and effectual in his own
nature. In short, to the Satanic worshiper, the Devil has
attained godhead and in his own right he is the deity himself. He inculcates his own morality, which runs counter to
the old traditional beliefs, the ancient appraisal of acts and
thoughts and intentions.

Hence, as a devout and passionate disciple of the Fiend, the Satanist will profess a new, a rebellious credo. Whatever recalls or touches on Christian doctrine is tainted. Whatever is opposed to such doctrine is true and real. Destroy then all Christian concepts. Ridicule Christian ceremonials, liturgies, rituals. Break down the inhibitory barriers of the established religion. Act in every sense in directions opposed to the ethics of Christianity. Be not afraid. There are no binding laws for the Satanist, except the laws of the negative, the laws of Satan.

In the tenebrous history of the arcane arts, there have appeared various sects, secret societies, individuals that acquired a legendary or warranted reputation for Satanism and involvement in diabolic performances.

In the first century A.D., Apollonius of Tyana was known as a Neopythagorean philosopher. Interested in occultism, he traveled widely, as far as India. During his travels he taught philosophy and also acquired vast esoteric knowledge. It was said of him that he possessed miraculous powers, and he was believed to have encountered demons and vampires and other monstrosities. By clairvoyance he foretold the date of the death of the Roman Emperor Domitian. In Asia Minor, temples were erected to him as the greatest thaumaturgist of his time. Finally, however, he was brought to trial in Rome, when the imperial decree forbade divination. Apollonius's reputation as a thaumaturgist grew into medieval legend, and he became the prototype of the Archmagician.

In the fourth century A.D., a certain Jewish scholar named Zambri was likewise considered a powerful magician. It was said that he had killed a ferocious bull merely by uttering the divine mystic name. But it was assumed that Zambri had a Satanic alliance.

In the eleventh century, in northern Italy, the Cathari

equated God with Satan. Hence they repudiated the precepts of the Old Testament, practiced unnatural vice, and indulged in sexual promiscuity.

Artephius, a mystic and a hermetic, was one of the early seekers of the Philosopher's Stone. He flourished in the twelfth century. He declared that he was over one thousand years old. He also professed to have visited the Nether Regions. His treatise, *The Art of Prolonging Human Life,* was published in Paris in 1612.

Arnold of Villanova, a thirteenth-century physician, practiced alchemy and the black arts. For these purposes he traveled throughout Europe and also in Africa. He was credited with the ability to converse with the Satanic forces. As a physician, he prescribed magic philtres for his patients and used occult conjurations in his treatments.

The Bogomils, called the "children of Satanael," were a heretical religious sect that flourished in the Balkans from the tenth to the fifteenth century. They first appeared in Bulgaria. Their name stemmed from their founder, a priest named Bogomil. Their central teaching was that the material, visible world was created by the Devil. They spurned the cross. They rejected Christian miracles, baptism, and the entire hierarchical organization of the Christian church.

In France, the Albigensians were a heretical sect suspected of communication with the Fiend. In 1299 some fifteen thousand Albigensians were massacred in a crusade instituted by Pope Innocent III.

During the twelfth century, another religious sect rose into notoriety. Founded by Peter Waldo in 1177 in France, the Waldensians, stigmatized as heretical, were denounced by the Pope. For some two centuries they lived secluded lives, in Piedmont, on the Alpine slopes. They acquired a widespread reputation as sorcerers, cannibals, and Satanists.

The Knights Templars, the medieval chivalric Order, were brought to trial on charges of Satanism. They were accused of worshiping the Devil in the shape of a cat and of performing obscene and sacrilegious acts that defiled Christian beliefs.

The medieval centuries were marked by prolonged conflicts between Christian faith and paganism. Paganism meant the ancient mysteries, the secret cults involving strange rites, diabolic practices, obscene allegiance. A figure that achieved prominence in this respect was a certain Guillaume de Paris. With demoniac aid, as his popular reputation ran, he had produced a number of statues endowed with speech.

In the fifteenth century, a heretical sect calling themselves Brethren of the Cross appeared in Germany. They practiced nocturnal orgies and professed an adoration of Satan.

In the reign of Henry IV of France, a certain Ansuperomin was known as a sorcerer who frequented and participated in the Sabbat rituals.

One of the most dominant personalities in the entire field of the Occult Arts was Paracelsus.

Philippus Aureolus Paracelsus (c. 1490–1541), whose real name was Theophrastus Bombastus von Hohenheim, was a famous physician, alchemist, and occultist. He was born in Switzerland, and his fame spread throughout medieval Europe.

He investigated diseases arising from work in mines and, contrary to traditional medical practice, propounded his own theories of treatment. Forced to leave his university position, he practiced in Germany and finally in Austria.

In his medical practice he used chiromancy, occult rites, and alchemical experiments. He considered man to be compounded of three bodies: elemental or physical, sidereal or astral, and illumined, that is, endowed with the spark of God.

Paracelsus also prognosticated, using a magic speculum or mirror. He left specific directions for making such a speculum.

In his later years he degenerated, giving way to debauchery and vagabondage. He frequently invoked the spirits of the dead by necromantic means. He declared that when in doubt he consulted his familiar, a demon. This familiar he carried about with him, in the hilt of his sword.

Agrippa von Nettesheim (1486–1535), whose full name was Henry Cornelius Agrippa von Nettesheim, was generally known as Agrippa. Physician, soldier, and occultist, he experienced fame and wealth and prestige, then sank into poverty and obscurity. He traveled throughout Europe, and also in England. He was a necromancer and had as an attendant a demon in the form of a black dog. He wrote a treatise on magic and the occult arts under the title of *De Occulta Philosophia*.

Dr. John Dee (1537–1608) was a noted Elizabethan mathematician and an M.A. of Cambridge University. He made important contributions in navigation and astronomy. He left a great deal of autobiographical material, particularly dealing with his professional work. His interests spread to occult subjects, notably alchemy and astrology. For casting horoscopes and practicing magic against Mary Queen of England he suffered imprisonment. He was called "the late Queen's conjurer." In 1604 he made a petition to be cleared of the accusation of being a karcist. Later on, he was sent on government service to the Continent. There he formed an acquaintanceship with Edward Kelley, who claimed to be a magician and a necromancer. Dr. Dee was reputed to be a Satanist himself and to practice necromancy. There was no specific evidence of such performances, but the legend persisted and grew. On the other hand, he had "visions." He wrote an account of his conversations with angels through a medium.

Dr. Dee is the author of *Liber Mysteriorum*—The Book of Mysteries—in seventeen books. *A Diary* is autobiographical, and his *Compendious Rehearsall* is a listing of his other works, some forty-nine at that time.

One of his occult properties was a magic mirror that he used in crystallomancy. This mirror is now in the possession of the Dublin Museum.

In an old print Edward Kelley and Dr. Dee are shown in a necromantic performance. The scene is a graveyard by night. Both figures stand in the magic circle, in which are inscribed the names of the demons Rael, Miraton, Bael, Rex, Tarmiel. They have been invoked to lend their fiendish aid. The magic wand that is the peculiar property of the magician is held by Kelley, who also holds open an occult grimoire. His companion upholds a torch. Before them stands the spirit that they have conjured. The figure is still wrapped in its grave-clothes.

The Count of St. Germain was a French adventurer and occultist, for some time attached to the diplomatic service of Louis XV. He was a versatile character, interested in painting and music, and was reputed to know some dozen languages, including Arabic and Chinese. Claiming possession of the Philosopher's Stone, he confirmed his claim by his vast wealth. He also studied the occult arts and boasted of the power of invisibility. He also asserted that he had found, in a specific health diet, the Elixir of Life. As alleged testimony to this discovery, it was believed that he was at least two thousand years old. The putative date of his death is given as 1784, but there was a strange belief that after the date of his assumed death he was able to correspond with living members of the French nobility.

Pietro Mora, a Milanese physician who flourished in the seventeenth century, was also reputed to be a karcist. He dabbled in astrology and experimented in alchemical researches. In the popular view he was considered an effective magician and an adherent of Satanism.

William Beckford (1759–1844), the English novelist and voluptuary, was the author of the Gothic tale *Vathek*. He was fabulously wealthy and traveled widely. In a palace with a two-hundred-and-sixty-foot tower, he lived in isolated splendor. Apart from being a collector and a bibliophile, he interested himself in demonology and Oriental magic.

Edward Bulwer Lytton (1803–1873), English dramatist, diplomat, and novelist, was the author of an occult tale entitled *The Coming Race*. He was said to have been intensely interested in thaumaturgic operations.

In the latter decades of the nineteenth-century, Samuel Liddell Mathers, occultist, became head of the secret Order of the Golden Dawn, an esoteric club. Mathers, who lived in Paris, was a votary of the cult of Isis, the ancient Egyptian goddess who, among other functions, presided over the magic arts. Mathers's home was consequently decorated in the style of an Egyptian temple, where he was accustomed to invoke the goddess in ceremonial robes. Mathers translated and edited a number of occult treatises, among them the grimoires *The Key of Solomon* and the *Book of Sacred Magic of Abramelin the Sage*.

Of all the sinister characters who have been concerned with the occult arts, the most recent and most notorious figure is Edward Aleister Crowley, who in his writings never used his first name. As a contemporary of Mathers, he was a bitter rival for the leadership of the Order of the Golden Dawn.

Crowley was remarkable for his talents and also for his perversities. An artist and a traveler and mountain-climber, he was alsó a poet, a drug addict, an excellent chess player, and a magician.

Born in 1875, he died in 1947. The son of a brewer, he inherited a vast fortune, which he rapidly dissipated. He was educated at a famous public school, Malvern, and at Cambridge University. His wife, Rose Kelly, had clairvoyant powers, and he used her as a medium in invoking spirits. In conformity with his dark career and his own wishes, in the crematorium chapel at Brighton, at his death, his dedicated followers performed a Satanic ritual. A pagan litany was chanted to his memory, ending with the cry to the ancient pagan deity: Io Pan, Io Pan, Io Pan. In his esoteric *persona*, Crowley called himself Frater Perdurabo: Brother I Shall Endure.

He was reputed to have reached the foulest and most bestial nadir in all the variations of the Black Arts. He achieved the climax of his macabre and ghastly career by proclaiming himself a Satanist. He called himself the Beast 666. The reference was to *Revelation* 13:18:

Here is wisdom. Let him that hath understanding count the number of the beast: for it is the number of a man; and his number is six hundred threescore and six.

He claimed that he was a reincarnation of Eliphas Lévi, the French occultist, and of another occultist, Edward Kelley. Kelley himself, a magician, necromancer, an adept in divination, especially crystallomancy, was associated with Dr. John Dee, the mathematician and karcist.

Rejecting Christian doctrine and traditions, Crowley established a mystic cult. Its essential principle was based on a total repudiation of orthodox Christianity. As a student of the Kabala, the mystic, Hebraic "hidden wisdom," Crowley absorbed the major expository treatise of the Kabala, namely, the *Zohar*, the Book of Splendor.

Crowley had already shown his perversities. He had become a member of another cult called The Order of the Golden Dawn. The Golden Dawn had branches or lodges in London, Paris, Edinburgh, and other cities. Among its members were Arthur Machen and Algernon Blackwood, both noted writers of mystic stories.

Later, Crowley founded his own esoteric club, the Astrum Argentinum—The Silver Star. Here he expanded his activities as the Beast 666. His rituals, which attracted and long enlisted women, were compounded of blasphemous ceremonies of the type of the Black Mass, goetic performances, demoniac liturgies, and invariably sexual orgies. In London he founded a Satanic temple.

Crowley traveled with a companion in North Africa. There he practiced his black skills. By means of rituals and invocations drawn from the medieval Grimoire of Honorius and the manuscript known as The Lemegeton or The Lesser Key of Solomon, containing the seventy-two names of the demoniac hierarchy, he conjured the diabolic and protean form of the powerful fiend Choronzon.

In 1920 he set up his headquarters at the Sacred Abbey of Thelema, in Sicily. In cooperation with his two mistresses, he exercised his unspeakable abominations until his bestialities became a byword. Expelled from Italy, then from France, he roamed through Portugal, Germany, England. In World War I, he moved to the United States, where he wrote anti-British propaganda.

He edited an occult magazine, *The Equinox*. He also published a considerable amount of poetry, permeated by sexuality, and dramatic pieces marked by occult symbolism and esoteric views.

His first treatise on magic was *The Book of the Law*. He wrote an occult novel entitled *The Moonchild*. Another of his books was *The Book of Lies*. His final work was *The Last Ritual*. His dramas include *Mortadello, The Savior*. His chief work was a treatise under the title *Magick in Theory and Practice,* which was published in Paris in 1929, the author's name appearing as the Master Therion. In general, Crowley's writings deal with ceremonial magic, Oriental mysticism, and numerology. One of his manuals, the *Liber Samekh,* is a ritualistic handbook.

Once Crowley was invited to deliver a lecture at Oxford on Gilles de Rais, the Satanist, but the lecture was banned, although it was published later on.

The Spirit of Solitude is Crowley's autobiography. Later, he re-antichristened it, as he said, under the title of *The Confessions of Aleister Crowley*.

Crowley appears as the leading character in W. Somerset Maugham's *The Magician*. An absorbing biography of the Satanist was published by John Addington Symonds, the art critic.

Occult techniques, cases of possession, Satanic beliefs and performances have not vanished from the human scene. The Demon appears unexpectedly, in his own time, in unforeseen circumstances. The Devil, as the old adage ran, bides his time. In 1788, for instance, in England, there was a report of an epileptic who in a fit of drunkenness clamored in the streets that he was possessed. Exorcism was attempted, and after prolonged efforts a swarm of devils were said to have issued from the victim's mouth. Old pagan superstitions, rites, conjurations, the weird apparatus of the karcist and the witch still survive, largely under cover, in protective secrecy. They become public knowledge only when lurid or brutal or bestial sensations create a startled furor. Such things, it is then asserted, cannot be. But the participants themselves know that they can be, and are.

XII

SATAN IN LITERATURE

LITERATURE HAS always approached Satan with interest—sometimes with excessive and biased interest—often even with a certain respect, and at times actually with veneration. But never with indifference.

The Archfiend has not always been vilified. He has been the subject of apologetics, of casuistic condonement, even of forgiveness. He has been raised to the heights. He has been placed side by side with the Divinity, and not infrequently has even overshadowed that divinity. Wherever there has been bloodshed, in the dolorous chronicles of history, in contemporary life, wherever violence, political turmoil, rape, vice in all its permutations and outrage have manifested themselves, there the Devil has been abroad, has demonstrated, by his monstrous incitements, his bestialities, his primal smoldering antipathies. All his bitter rancor has been distilled into his dynamic antagonisms to men, and his roster of atrocities is a perpetual testimony to his prowess and his sense of security and assurance.

Thus he becomes a *persona,* acknowledged in poetry and drama, in philosophical expositions and theological dialectic, and also in the more popular types of literature. Joseph Petrus Borel, a nineteenth-century Frenchman who dabbled in letters, had a vast respect for the Demon. He called himself le lycanthrope—the wolf-man—and he experienced many misadventures during his complicated life. At one time he actually founded an eccentric journal under the name of *Satan*. The Fiend had at last entered the Fourth Estate. But the periodical, unlike Satan himself, was short-lived.

Giosuè Carducci (1835–1907), the Italian poet, in his volume of verses under the title of *Satana e Polemiche Sataniche*, glorifies the Devil.

George Bernard Shaw, with his wry cynicism, brought Don Juan down to Hell. Shaw gives the Devil more than his due merits. The Devil exclaims:

You come to us from earth, full of the prejudices and terrors of that priest-ridden place. You have heard me ill spoken of; and yet, believe me, I have hosts of friends there.

It is true—he continues—that the world cannot get on without me; but it never gives me credit for that: in its heart it mistrusts and hates me. Its sympathies are all with misery, with poverty, with starvation of the body and of the heart. I call on it to sympathize with joy, with love, with happiness, with beauty.

Shaw's *The Devil's Disciple* confirmed his diabolical concern. And quite evidently the Devil has sometimes been painted too darkly. For in Shakespeare's *Twelfth Night* the Clown addresses Malvolio:

Fie, thou dishonest Satan! I call thee by the most modest terms; for I am one of those gentle ones that will use the devil himself with courtesy.

The Voyage of St. Brendan is a medieval account of a **narrative, with symbolic undertones, by St. Brendan the**

Navigator, a sixth-century Irish Abbot. During the voyage to the Promised Land, along with some of his monks, he encounters strange adventures, miraculous scenes, and horrifying confrontations involving diabolic forces. But he survives by the strength of his righteousness.

In *Parsival*, Book 9, the hermit speaks to the knight about the contest between Lucifer and the Trinity. And the Trinity was always a point of issue with Satan.

Machiavelli has a story about the devil's marriage to a woman who, with the help of her mother, got the better of him. A similar theme appears in *The Devil's Mother-in-Law*, by Fernan Caballero, a nineteenth-century Spanish novelist.

Monk Lewis, the early nineteenth-century English novelist, is noted for his Gothic tales. In *Ambrosius, or The Monk*, he relates how a devout cleric was ruined by a succubus.

At times the Devil displays violent animosity against a particular monastery, against a noted cathedral. So Longfellow, in the prologue of Part 2 of *The Golden Legend*, presents Lucifer, with the Powers of the Air, making an assault on Strasburg Cathedral. Satan's purpose is to tear away the cross from the spire, to desecrate the dead, hurl down the bells, smash the casements:

Night and storm. Lucifer, with the Powers of the Air, trying to tear down the Cross.

Lucifer

Hasten! hasten!
O ye spirits!
From its station drag the ponderous
Cross of iron, that to mock us
Is uplifted high in air!

Voices

Oh, we cannot!
For around it

All the Saints and Guardian Angels
Throng in legions to protect it;
They defeat us everywhere!

The Bells

Laudo Deum verum!
Plebem voco!
Congrego clerum!

Lucifer

Lower! lower!
Hover downward!
Seize the loud, vociferous bells, and
Clashing, clanging, to the pavement
Hurl them from their windy tower!

Voices

All thy thunders
Here are harmless!
For these bells have been anointed,
And baptized with holy water!
They defy our utmost power.

The Bells

Defunctos ploro!
Pestem fugo!
Festa decoro!

Lucifer

Shake the casements!
Break the painted
Panes, that flame with gold and crimson;
Scatter them like leaves of Autumn,
Swept away before the blast!

Voices

O, we cannot!
The Archangel
Michael flames from every window,

With the sword of fire that drove us
Headlong, out of heaven, aghast!

The Bells

Funera plango!
Fulgura frango!
Sabbata pango!

Lucifer

Aim your lightnings
At the oaken,
Massive, iron-studded portals!
Sack the house of God, and scatter
Wide the ashes of the dead!

Voices

Oh, we cannot!
The Apostles
And the Martyrs, wrapped in mantles,
Stand as warders at the entrance,
Stand as sentinels o'erhead!

The Bells

Excito lentos!
Dissipo ventos!
Paco cruentos!

Finally, Lucifer, frustrated, howls his humiliation:

Lucifer

Baffled! baffled!
Inefficient,
Craven spirits! leave this labor
Unto Time, the great Destroyer!
Come away, ere night is gone!

Voices

Onward! onward!
With the night-wind,

Over field and farm and forest,
Lonely homestead, darksome hamlet,
Blighting all we breathe upon!

In the sequel, through scenes in castle and farmhouse, in cloisters and domestic chambers, among princelings and scholars and monks, the Devil, sometimes in the guise of a priest, marches on his insidious way. But:

The Kingdom still remaineth!
However Satan may rage and roar.

Mario Rapisardi, the Italian poet who died in 1912, is the author of the epic *Il Lucifero*. Strange how Satan's personality winds itself into song and ballad, into farce and drama, into religious mystery plays and riotous sympotic chants, into ghostly narratives and domestic comedies. Ernst Theodore Amadeus Hoffman (1776–1822), the German composer and writer, produced a Satanic tale under the name of *The Devil's Elixir*. Tasso's epic, *Jerusalem Delivered*, describes the ancient horrendous forms assumed by the Archfiend's demons.

The Demon appears in Byron's *Manfred*, as well as in his *Cain*. Manfred is a drama in the Faust tradition—not an unusual situation, for Byron himself had a touch of diablerie in his composition and was not unacquainted with Satanic ways. That dark, melancholic spirit, Edgar Allan Poe, saw Satanic movements and gestures and approaches in every phase of human conduct, and with his chilling perversity he achieved a laudation of the Evil Spirit in *The Imp of the Perverse*. But perhaps his most awesome venture is *Silence: A Fable*, that begins with the Devil's command to listen and ends, on a wild occult note, with the lynx, creeping out of its eternal tomb and casting itself at Satan's feet.

In Canto 34 of Dante's *Inferno*, the Fiend stands domi-

nantly, in the midst of those who have betrayed their bene-
factors. The nineteenth-century French novelist and critic,
Barbey d'Aurevilly, is the author of *L'Ensorcelée*—The Bewitched—as well as *Les Diaboliques,* a collection of six short
stories illustrating the powerful influence of evil. Arthur
Rimbaud too, that restless, exotic figure, entered the Fiend's
domain with *Une Saison en Enfer,* a symbolic account of his
relations with the poet Paul Verlaine.

In the Bibliothèque Nationale in Paris, there is a section
known as l'Enfer, devoted to esoteric and occult literature.
Also in Paris, in the Bibliothèque de l'Arsenal de Paris, one
of the departments contains manuscripts and treatises on
Satanism, Black Magic, and related subjects.

Charles Baudelaire (1821–1867), the French poet, addressed the Devil with a personal plea:

O Satan, prends pitié de ma longue misère!
O Satan, take pity on my long wretchedness!

In Rabelais there is Papefiguière with his Devil.

Joost van den Vondel (1587–1679) was the greatest national
Dutch poet and playwright. His drama *Lucifer,* published in
1654 and translated into English as late as 1898, makes Satan
the central character. The play is in classical form, and was
modeled on Greek tragic drama.

Alain René Lesage (1668–1747), was a French novelist and
dramatist. He is the author of *Le Diable Boiteux.* Both the
title and the general plot of the book were borrowed from
a similar novel, in Spanish, *El Diablo Cojuelo,* by Luiz
Velez de Guevara. So that, particularly in fiction, but not
exclusively so, of course, the Satanic theme knows no regional
frontiers.

Jacques Cazette, an eighteenth-century French poet who
met his death in the French Revolution, is the author of
Le Diable Amoureux—The Devil in Love.

Thus, in the course of his relationships with human beings, the Devil assumes human domestic habits. He marries. He has a daughter. He is driven from home by a shrewish wife. He is badgered and harassed and hounded like any average husband. And Satan does not hesitate to recount these depressing circumstances. In the early nineteenth century a certain French writer, Frederic Soulié, produced *Les Mémoires du Diable,* a kind of last literary confession of the Fiend before passing into oblivion.

In *The Wonderful History of Peter Schlemihl,* by Adelbert von Chamisso (1781–1838), the Devil appears, and steals the hero's shadow.

Victor Hugo, that prolific and flamboyant poet, envisages the redemption of Satan in his unfinished *La Fin de Satan.* The motif is not new in itself, for through the centuries beliefs were prevalent that Satan had been restored, by the Divinity's mercy, to his rightful position in the hierarchy of heaven.

In this connection may be mentioned the Yezidi, who have been called "devil-worshipers." The Yezidi form a dwindling community inhabiting Kurdistan. Their religious center is near Mosul. They consider that they were not descended from Adam, and they maintain an exclusive social aloofness. This heretical Islamic sect probably stems from Christian concepts, but was influenced also by the cults of the Near East. The name derives from Yazid, angel, their chief divine figure. They believe that the Evil Spirit is no longer essentially evil, since he has been pardoned for his misdeeds. Later on, they declare, he was placed among the highest angels. This view was virtually held by Dante, who considers Satan, in his primal condition, as "the paragon of all creation," touched with nobility and grace, in addition to physical perfection. Yazid, called Melek Ta'us—King of Peacocks—rules the universe with six other angels.

Akin to the Yezidi were the Luciferans, a medieval sect

of heretics. Their view was that Lucifer had been expelled from heaven unjustly and that ultimately Lucifer, aided by his own angels, would be victorious.

Satan's rule could not be eternal. His prestige was terminal. That was the view of St. Bernard. He felt that the Devil's power was shortly to end, sometime in the twelfth century in which St. Bernard lived. "The Devil," he said, "is not yet in Hell fire, but the fire is ready to receive him, and he has only a short time left, in which to commit evil."

In that same twelfth century, miracle and mystery plays were very popular as entertainment linked with religious instruction. In one such mystery play, *Le Jeu de Adam,* the Devil has a prominent role. Satan, exhausted, actually prayed for death. In *La Mort du Diable*—The Death of Satan—a poem by Maxime du Camp, the nineteenth-century French journalist, Satan does meet his end. Imaginatively the poem conceives the Fiend's final collapse. All the Devil's machinations, his calamitous intrusions into human affairs, are brought to an end, like his own ultimate downfall and death. For even Satan can tire of his practices. In the final issue he becomes a suppliant himself, begging God, as one of the ancient pagan gods begged the Keeper of Hades, for the blessing of death.

For a thousand years, declares *Revelation* 20:7, Satan shall be bound:

And when the thousand years are expired, Satan shall be loosed out of his prison.

But the day of Satan's final destruction will come. On the day of the Last Judgment, Jesus will say to the wicked:

Depart from me, ye cursed, into everlasting fire, prepared for the devil and his angels.

MATTHEW 25:4

In Dostoevsky's *The Brothers Karamazov,* Ivan is confronted by Satan, who appears as a shabby-genteel figure, black-haired, bearded. That is the Devil's usual image in the newer fictional approach to the Evil One. His human, almost pitiful appearance is contrasted with the potency of his operations and the tremendous impacts that he exerts on man, who is fundamentally frail and insecure.

The poets seem to have a special leaning toward the diabolic personality. He appears in the poetry of Alfred de Vigny, in Lermontov's *The Demon,* in Baudelaire's *Les Litanies de Satan.*

John Webster, the dramatist and contemporary of Shakespeare, is the author of a tragicomedy entitled *The Devil's Law Case.*

One of the most monumental creative works is *The Demons,* by the Austrian novelist Heimito von Doderer. The book, on which the author worked for some thirty years, was published in 1956. It presents a spacious canvas of characters —historians and novelists, soldiers, factory workers, villains, bank directors, murderers, various types of women—and the theme is the Sophoclean insidiousness of fate and the demoniac interpenetration of men's ways through life.

In the early nineteenth century, E. H. Bierstadt produced a drama entitled *The Mysterious Stranger.* It was, in French, *Satan, ou le Diable à Paris.*

Another fiendish title was *Satan,* by C. P. Cranch. It was published in 1874, and although it was a poem the author called it a libretto, because to him it suggested a musical composition.

C. S. Henry was the author of *Satan as a Moral Philosopher* —an unusual role for the Fiend.

Satan Chained was a poem by a certain Professor N. Dunn.

J. W. Green, in 1844, published a poem in five books

under the title of *Satan Conquered, or The Son of God Victorious.*

Satan in Search of a Wife, by Charles Lamb, is a whimsical piece in verse, disclosing, as the author says, the whole process of his courtship and marriage and who danced at the wedding. He makes the Fiend into a very domestic character, with human characteristics.

Jules Michelet, the French historian, published in 1863 *La Sorcière,* an account of occultism. Michelet also wrote along the same lines a survey of Satanism and its practices.

The Russian novelist Dmitri Merejkowski introduced impressive descriptions of Satanic rites in his *Romance of Leonardo da Vinci.* His wife, Zinaida Nikolaevna, also a novelist, published in 1910 *The Devil's Doll.*

Following this domesticated line, F. M. Fitzpatrick published in 1955 *Satan Had a Daughter.*

In 1920 Violet Paget came out with *Satan the Waster.* It contains a *Prologue in Hell.*

And, of course, in the 1960's Satan figured prominently in the novel (and later the movie) *Rosemary's Baby.*

In the genre of the short story, Satan has received merited attention. He has been the prolific subject of tales by Pirandello and Israel Zangwill, Thackeray, Kipling, and Washington Irving. Hawthorne noted his possibilities, as did the British poet laureate John Masefield, and Balzac, Gorky, Bret Harte, Lord Dunsany, Arthur Machen. August Derleth and H. P. Lovecraft have approached Satan in a deeply occult sense, stressing the awesomeness of his presence, the unspeakable terror of an encounter. Anatole France, Conan Doyle, J. K. Bangs (author also of *The Houseboat on the Styx*), Hilaire Belloc and Le Fanu, Conrad, Algernon Blackwood, Baring-Gould, A. E. Coppard, M. R. James, and W. W. Jacobs have each found some unique feature, a fresh angle in Satanic history.

The tales themselves may be satirical or farcical, mystical.

tremulous with unutterable secrets, sometimes touched with a profound undefined fear of diabolic reality, of demoniac possibilities.

The following list, arranged alphabetically by authors, includes recent short stories as well as others of an earlier date. Some are the work of noted writers, while others appear to be more lightly thrown off as more or less whimsical tours de force. They all treat the Satanic theme with ingenuity and vision, occasionally even with a certain sympathetic and compassionate approach. In a general sense, they underline the unpredictable and sometimes mystical operations of his Infernal Majesty.

Atherton, G. F. H. "When the Devil was Well"

Balzac, H. de. "The Devil's Disciple"
Bangs, J. K. "The Midnight Visitor"
Barrie, J. M. "Farewell to Miss Julie Logan"
Bécquer, G. A. "The Devil's Cross"
Belloc, H. "The Story of St. Dunstan"
Beerbohm, Max. "Enoch Soames"
Bester, A. "Will You Wait?"
Blackwood, A. "The Secret Worship"
Bloch, R., "The Hell-bound Train"
Bond, N. S. "Saint Mulligan"
Buchan, John. "The Watcher by the Threshold"

Caballero, F. "The Devil's Mother-in-Law"
Caldecott, A. "His Name Was Legion"
Clifford, H. C. "The Ghoul"
Coleridge, M. E. "The Devil at the Guildhall"
Collier, J. "Halfway to Hell"
Collier, J. "The Possession of Angela Bradshaw"
Collier, J. "The Fallen Star"
Conrad, Joseph. "The Inn of the Two Witches"
Coppard, A. E. "The Devil in the Churchyard"

Dean, G. "The Devil's Bed"
Derleth, A. "Satan's Mask"
Derleth, A. "He Shall Come"
Derleth, A. "Mr. Ames' Devil"
Derleth, A. "Logoda's Heads"
Doble, C. C. "St. Christopher and the Devil"
Dunsany, Lord. "A Deal with the Devil"
Dyke, H. van. "The Devil at Sea"

France, Anatole. "Satan's Tongue-pie"

Garnett, R. "The Potion of Lao-Tsze"
Garnett, R. "The Poet of Panopolis"
Garnett, R. "The Claw"
Garnett, R. "The Bell of St. Euschemon"
Garnett, R. "The Demon Pope"
Garnett, R. "Madame Lucifer"
Gogol, N. "St. John's Eve"
Gorky, M. "The Devil"
Green, P. "Supper for the Dead"
Grimm, J. and W. "The Devil Turned Pleader"

Harte, B. "The Devil and the Broker"
Hawthorne, N. "The Devil in Manuscript"
Horgan, P. "The Devil in the Desert"
Housman, L. "Devil Help Us!"
Howard, R. E. "Black Canaan"
Howard, R. E. "The Black Stone"
Hughes, R. A. W. "The Stranger"

Irving, W. "The Devil and Tom Walker"
Irwin, M. "The Book"

Jacobi, C. "The Satanic Piano"
Jacobs, W. W. "Breaking a Spell"
James, M. R. "Whistle and I'll Come to You"
James, M. R. "Casting the Runes"

Keller, G. "The Fat of the Cat"
Kipling, R. "The Devil and the Deep Sea"
Kutner, H. "The Threshold"

Lagerkvist, P. "The Lift that Went Down to Hell"
Le Fanu, J. S. "The Sexton's Adventure"
Leroux, G. "In Letters of Fire"
Lille, B. "The Devil's Pit"
Lovecraft, H. O. "The Horror at Red Hook"

Maginn, A. "The City of the Demons"
Mann, F. A. "The Devil in a Nunnery"
Marquis, D. "Satan Goes to Church"
Masefield, J. "The Devil and the Old Man"
Maturin, C. R. "Melmoth the Wanderer"
Morgan, B. "The Devils of Po Sung"

O'Sullivan, V. "The Bargain of Rupert Grange"

Packard, F. L. "The Devil and All His Works"
Peretz, I. L. "The Eighth Circle of Gehenna"
Peretz, I. L. "The Lust for Clothes"
Perkins, F. B. "The Devil-puzzlers"
Pirandello, L. "The Evil Spirit"
Poe, E. A. "The Devil in the Belfry"
Poe, E. A. "Bon-Bon"
Poe, E. A. "Never Bet the Devil Your Head"
Powys, T. F. "The Devil"

Quiller-Couch, A. T. "The Horror on the Stair"

Rassell, W. C. "The Midnight Visitor"
Rudwin, M. J. (ed.) "Devil Stories"

Sabatini, R. "A Night of Witchcraft"
Sanders, W. P. "The Pact"
Seabrook, W. B. "The Witch's Vengeance"
Seinius, I. "The Bishop and the Devil"
Simms, W. G. "Comrade Weickhoff"

Smith, C. A. "The Return of the Sorcerer"
Smith, C. A. "Sadaster"
Smith, Lady E. F. "Satan's Circus"
Smith, W. "The Escape of Saemander"
Stevenson, R. L. "The Bottle Imp"

Thackeray, W. M. "The Devil's Wager"
Thomas, T. L. "Satan's Passage"
Twain, M. "The Mysterious Stranger"

Weston, G. "The Devil Has the Moon"
Whitehead, H. "West India Lights"

Zangwill, I. "Satan Mekatrig"

In the drama, Ibsen's *Peer Gynt* struck a new note, freshening up and bringing into actuality old Nordic sagas, a legendary aura of occult motifs: the Devil in the nutshell, trolls and witches, goblins and gnomes, Peer's encounters with the Button Moulder and the Thin Person, the Great Invisible One.

Philip James Bailey, an English poet who died in 1902, produced a poetic drama in which Lucifer has a prominent part. The theme itself is based on the Faust legend.

Robert Graves, the English poet, has a whimsical, cynical poem under the name of *The Devil's Advice to Story-Tellers*, which suggests devilish casuistic tricks of mixing truth and falsehood.

It is noteworthy that the theme of Hell and its inmates and Satan and his ministrants recurs with such frequency in poems and plays, or in contexts where diabolical atmospheres are treated by hints and brief but pregnant innuendoes. Satan is there, misdirecting frail, puzzled, vicious humans, creating complexities that end in damnation. He is not to be forgotten. He is too involved in the realities of human life and thought to take a respite, to burke any of his functions.

In films, the Fiend has been playing in the front line of

action. His visual image, projected repeatedly on the screen, has left its impress on the mind of the general public. He has become a cliché, a household word. He is no longer a subject of theological or academic discussion. He is no longer a concept, a myth, a traditional symbol. He is a palpable, material creature, who inspires horror and terror in men, who creates turmoil without reason, devastation, and agony. He is furtively, and then again openly present on human occasions. And he involves his demons together with humans in all sorts of malefic situations.

Among Satanic films that have appeared in this country and on the Continent may be listed these presentations:

The Devil
The Magician
The Black Cat
The Devil Commands
The Devil Doll
The Inferno
The Golem
The Sand Merchant
The Devil's Circus
The Devil's Assistant
The Devil's Manor
The Student of Prague
The Seventh Victim
The Sorrows of Satan
Seven Footprints to Satan
Faust
Rosemary's Baby

EPILOGUE

DEEP DOWN in his murky vaulted chambers, Satan was holding his monthly conference. He sat at his ebony desk with an agenda before him. He adjusted his horn-rimmed spectacles and looked around.

He pressed a button. Instantly a small furry creature, tail neatly tucked behind it, appeared.

"Your Satanic Majesty."

"Call Abigor."

In a trice Abigor stood before him, a gigantic, dark-winged demon.

"Your report?"

"Beg to report, your Imperial Majesty, as of this moment. The paperbacks are flourishing beyond belief."

"Don't use that last word again."

"Sorry, sir, I forgot."

"Continue."

"All the tales are dedicated to sorcery, potions for doing away with humans, necromancy, divination, the Sabbat, and so on. Newspapers, television, and other media are all taking up the subject. We're in."

Satan gave a chuckle. "Good. So I'm back in full force again, eh? No more of the old nonsense: Satanas, retro me. It's forward now. We've got them in our grasp. Satan Redivivus! It's high time too. We lost quite a lot last century. Well, good work, Abigor. You can stir the cauldron this weekend. It's the suburbanites' turn."

"The men and women you mentioned?"

"The whole boiling lot." Satan smiled at his own pun.

"Thanks, your Majesty."

Satan pressed the button once more.

Shabriri promptly appeared, the History of Occultism under his scaly arm.

"What's that?"

"I'm just brushing up on some techniques, your Majesty."

"Anything new?"

"The gods are dead. They admit it now. They're calling for you."

Satan nodded.

"The times are tremendously propitious," went on Shabriri. "Religion has crumbled away. Men are disillusioned. Faith is gone. New cults every day. Almost a replica of those last dying days of the Roman Empire. Remember, your Majesty?"

"Oh, yes. That fellow Juvenal did a good job for us."

"Cults are sweeping in from the Orient every day. Politics are putrescent. Sex is rampant. No domestic morality. No affection. No good will among people. Nothing but suspicion, hatred, barbarism, war, bombs, invasions, sedition, treason, mass murders, adultery, incest—the new games, violence, pederasty, bestiality. The whole lot."

Satan rubbed his horny hands. A devilish gleam came into his eyes, and he broke into diabolical laughter. "Just our meat."

"A few feeble voices have been raised, but they mean nothing. It's the triumph of war and universal chaos and the glorification of evil."

He stopped, breathless.

"Well, what are we waiting for?" Satan asked. "Let's begin. Order mobilization."

"To hear is to obey," responded Shabriri, with an Oriental obeisance. "Long live your Majesty. Send us victorious. God save our Master. We'll celebrate your triumph."

Satan made a deprecating gesture. "Drink one on me, Shabriri, will you?" and he faded into an acrid sulphurous cloud. "More pollution," he sniffed, as the escalator whisked him down to the nether basement.